HOW TO BUY
MOBILE HOMES
Updated 2nd Edition

HOW TO BUY MOBILE HOMES

Updated 2nd Edition

The Unorthodox Guide to Capitalizing on a Hidden Niche in Real Estate Investing

ADRIAN SMUDE

ISBN: 979-8-9853746-9-8

A Gift for Readers

Gain access to free video training and your companion guide for this book along with other resources. Go to **Lifestyle-rei.com/free-bonus**

There you may also subscribe to my weekly articles on real estate investing, business, and mindset.

This isn't just a book about mobile homes. It's a book about freedom, growth, and believing in what's possible.

Disclaimer

The stories and content in the following chapters are from real-life experiences. This is what has worked for me and my peers. This book does not provide any promises or guarantees regarding the subject matters covered. I am not offering legal, accounting, or other professional services.

This book's information is not meant to replace the advice of a certified professional. You might find it all works for you, a few items work for you, or none of it works for you. Always comply with fair housing. Consult with your attorney, Certified Public Accountant (CPA), and other professional counsel. Sometimes the best deals are the ones we do not buy.

Trust but verify.

Contents

Foreword

Unless you have been living under a rock, you know that America has a problem regarding the affordability of housing. The American dream includes being able to own your own home on your own land. It has become much harder to do that over the last several years.

Most real estate investors overlook one of the most obvious solutions to the problem of affordable housing – the amazing opportunity with mobile homes on land. They are an attractive solution to America's housing affordability crisis.

While I have done a few real estate deals involving mobile homes, my knowledge pales in comparison to that of Adrian Smude. I believe he is currently the top educator and speaker on how to wisely and profitably invest in mobile homes on land.

I have the privilege of being a close, personal friend of Adrian. You learn a lot about someone when they are riding solo on a tandem bike but can still keep up with you on your own bike. Adrian is focused, disciplined, and motivated, and he brings all those skills to bear in his real estate investing and lifestyle business.

I highly recommend this book to anyone who is considering investing in mobile homes or real estate. He gives you what you need to know to determine if something is a good deal or not.

The knowledge contained herein will save you years of headaches and heartburn and will allow your mobile home investing to become far more profitable than if you tried to do it on your own. Ask me how I know!

Not only will this book teach you the things you must know and must avoid when investing in mobile homes, but Adrian is a gifted marketer, who will also teach you how to market for both sellers and buyers. Those are two different skill sets that he lays out for you.

Most importantly, Adrien shows you how to do these deals with little of your own money and without banks being involved.

So, welcome to the interesting and profitable world of investing in mobile homes, brought to you by my friend Adrian Smude. Please enjoy profitably!

-Jeff Watson, Attorney, Best Selling Author, Educator
WatsonInvested.com

Preface

Welcome! Whether this is your first time reading or you're coming back for the revised edition, I'm grateful you're here. I wrote this book to help investors understand how to confidently invest in mobile homes. And judging by the generous five-star reviews, it seems to have delivered on that goal.

In fact, some people told me I gave away too much and that no one would need my video courses after reading this. But the opposite happened. I found that those who truly value the knowledge are even more eager to go deeper. The book became a steppingstone, not a replacement.

Something I didn't expect was the number of readers who told me they found the book **inspiring**. Not just helpful but motivational, especially to those who weren't in real estate yet. They saw my story and thought, "If he can do it, maybe I can too." This book isn't just about mobile homes and money. It's about life. That's why, in this updated edition, I wanted to give you a quick life update as well.

When I originally wrote this book, I was married and had my buying brand, **My Wife Buys Mobile Homes**. That brand was part of my identity and part of this book's story. Since then, life has changed. I'm now divorced and dating a wonderful woman. That season of my life has come to a close, but I'm incredibly grateful for the growth and clarity it gave me. So when you read references to "my wife" or to Erin, just know that was real and beautiful, and it was a previous chapter. Today, I operate as **Adrian Buys Mobile Homes**. I'm dating a incredible woman , and I'm proud of both who I was and who I'm becoming.

One of my deepest goals is to be authentic and relatable because I believe that's how we truly help each other. Not just through strategies and spreadsheets, but through honesty and connection.

Now, back to the book. I've made some updates to Chapter 5 on marketing and a few bonus chapters in this revision - one on **Fixing and Flipping** and another on **Mobile Homes in Parks**. These were inspired directly by reader feedback, so thank you for speaking up.

I also want to highlight something many readers missed the first time: the **Free Bonus Resources** I created just for you. Go to **https://www.lifestyle-rei.com/free-bonus** to grab yours. If you leave your email, you'll also get my weekly articles that are full of insights on mobile home investing, business, and mindset. Writing this book helped me realize that I love writing, and I've been doing it ever since.

One last thing, while writing this book, I learned something big about myself: **I'm dyslexic**. I always struggled in school and was placed in remedial classes. But no one ever called it what it was. I'm not sharing this to get sympathy. I'm sharing it to remind you: *You can do hard things*. If a dyslexic guy can write a book and build a real estate business, you can too.

Let's get started.
-   Adrain Smude

Introduction

This book is for you if you like taking action.

This book is for you if you are in search of a new asset class.

This book is for you if you are overwhelmed with traditional real estate.

This book is for you if you are looking for a higher return on your investment.

This book is not for you if you are looking to get rich overnight.

This book is not for you if you do not take action on what you learn.

This book is not for you if you are content in where you are financially.

Investing in mobile homes is my niche in real estate. I would never have discovered this niche if I had not been open-minded and asked seasoned investors my questions. I started my real estate journey as a tenant (and a terrible tenant at that!) with a stack of eviction notices from numerous landlords, which resulted in me living with my parents until I could close on a house of my own.

My first home purchase occurred in 2003 when banks loaned money to troublemakers like me without questions. After my purchase, I decided to move in with the same friends that had played a role in my eviction. This meant I lived for free because their rent paid my mortgage. I thought, *This is really cool!*

Unfortunately, my second house purchase was not so cool. I purchased it and lost a little each month, but I reassured myself, "It's okay. I'll refinance in a few years because the housing market is on fire!"

WRONG! A few years later, I let the house go as a short sale for less than 50% of my original purchase price. At that time I was embarrassed, but today I am grateful because this helped me become a conservative investor. After purchasing a few more houses, I remembered the short sale experience and thought the housing market was close to peaking. In hindsight I was wrong again because the housing market has been increasing in value for years since then.

Being wrong is one of the best things that has happened to me. I would not have found the niche of investing in mobile homes with land if it weren't for my previous short sale. It didn't take me long to realize I enjoy the cash flow from mobile homes more than the cash flow from traditional site-built homes. I was able to purchase many more mobile homes for the same amount of money as one site-built home. I've realized a few important things through my investment experience:

- I am a cash flow investor, not a speculator.
- I am a cash flow investor, not a fixer-and-flipper.
- I am a cash flow investor, not an appreciation investor.
- I look for the best return on my dollar for the least amount of work. This is how I created the lifestyle I have today.

One of my greatest accomplishments was enabling my wife, Erin, to retire at the age of 29. This freedom allowed her to find her most fulfilling place in the world. Erin's real passion is helping those in need at the most critical moments of their life. Erin spent most of 2020 and 2021 working across the US as a travel nurse, assisting with emergencies like COVID-19, hurricanes, and nursing shortages.

Freedom! Erin and I have put ourselves in a position where Erin can leave on a moment's notice to help those in need. Because I'm not consumed in our business, I am able to visit Erin often. We have found the feeling of true freedom is the ability to decide where we want to be and when, all while doing what we want! After taking action on this book's lessons, you too will be on your way to this freedom.

You'll gain confidence as you read—you'll learn how to purchase mobile homes with land, know the key items to look for in mobile home purchases, and understand how to finance your mobile home purchase. You'll also realize that I didn't have all the answers when I started, yet I took action, asked for help, and failed forward along my journey. Every time I take action, I do it with a wiser approach because I learn from my previous actions.

This book brings you through my journey to where I am today—being a confident investor and teacher in the niche of mobile homes with land. The business I created enables my wife and I to be geographically free, focusing on our passions of helping others, and spreading joy and happiness.

This book isn't a fluff sales pitch or get-rich scheme. Let's set some ground rules so you get the most out of the info presented:

1. You must have the goal to truly help people.
2. You must be willing to take action on what you learn.
3. You must be willing to adapt the information to your personality.
4. You must understand that your education never ends.

5. You must have a WHY that is bigger than "making money."

This book is a tool for you, and it's written in a way that I would have found helpful at the start of my real estate investing career. You'll find the common myths about mobile homes, everything you need to know to invest in mobile homes, and how you can have my lifestyle by taking action.

Mobile home myths busted

To upgrade your mindset, let's bust some myths.

Before we dive into the bulk of the content, let's check your mindset about mobile homes. The most important thing you can do to accelerate your success is to adopt the right frame of mind. If you believe these myths about mobile homes, the information in this book probably won't impact your actions. We don't want that because the goal is for you to take action using this book's insights.

Myth 1: All mobile homes are "trailer trash."

People make the difference. Not all mobile homes are "trailer trash." The structure of a home does not determine the quality of the neighborhood or the person(s) living in the structure. People make the difference. The neighbors collectively determine the quality of the neighborhood. You have wood frames, concrete, and mobile homes in both run-down areas and in prosperous areas. My wife and I don't purchase mobile homes in unsafe areas. There are many areas where mobile homes sell for the same price as a site-built home.

Location, location, location is what we've always heard about real estate. Location is the key distinction between investing in areas that might be considered full of "trailer trash" or "aluminum castles."

Myth 2: All mobile homes have lot rent.

It is not true that all mobile homes have *lot rent*, or additional fees for renting the space for the mobile home. Only homes where you do not own the land have lot rent. This typically occurs in a mobile home park where you pay the mobile home park owner a monthly fee (or lot rent) for the right to park your mobile home.

My wife and I mainly invest in mobile homes in which we own the home and the land. These can be in a neighborhood which are all mobile homes, and each person owns their land and home. Or it can be in the county where we own an acre of land with the mobile home.

Myth 3: All mobile homes are in age-restricted neighborhoods.

I have found that although there are many age-restricted neighborhoods with mobile homes, this is not the case for the majority. There are different types of age-restricted neighborhoods: condos, site-built single-family houses, apartments and, of course, mobile homes.

The best way to find the status is to ask the owner or title company. Age-restricted neighborhoods can be 40, 45, 50, or 55 years old and up. These rules change depending on the association or mobile home park owner.

I have seen it where only the mobile home owner must be of age, and I have seen it that everyone living in the home must be at age. At times the rules say that a set percentage in that community must be of age. An example would be 80% of the residents must be 45 years old or older.

I don't invest in age-restricted neighborhoods because there is a lack of demand in the summer when the snowbirds go home. If I was up North, I'd have a lack of demand in the winter when the snowbirds migrate south.

Myth 4: You must have a license to invest in mobile homes.

This is a two-part myth: some people think you need a real estate license or a mobile home dealer's license to be a mobile home investor. Both are false. You only need a real estate license if you plan to buy and sell mobile homes and land for other people. You only need a mobile home dealer's license if you plan to buy and sell just the mobile homes for other people.

I do not hold either license because my goal is to buy the mobile home for myself. Some of the most successful investors I know don't have either license. They don't need it, so neither do you!

Myth 5: Old mobile homes cannot be repaired.

I don't know where this myth came from, but it is no more true than saying an old house cannot be repaired. Just like a site-built house you take care of; you can repair and update a mobile home. If you don't do the proper maintenance, your mobile home will become condemned.

One of the nicest mobile homes I have seen was built in the 1960s, but there was almost nothing original in that home. The owners completely remodeled the home and took incredible care of the place. Yet one of the worst mobile homes I've been in was built in 2015, but it was in bad condition because the owners let the weather get to it. It wasn't profitable to bring the 2015 mobile home back to life because of the extensive water damage. The only reason I felt safe breathing in that mold-infested mobile home was because all of the windows were missing!

We have rebuilt a 1968 mobile home that many argued needed to be hauled to the dump. But because of the work we've put in, we're still getting cash flow today. It's possible to repair a mobile home to the point of profitability.

Myth 6: Mobile homes always go down in value.

This is not always true, but mobile homes don't appreciate the same as a site-built home. If you are referring only to the mobile home, the statement holds true. But a livable mobile home does not decrease to $0 in value. There is value to the person living in the mobile home because there is a roof over their head, and there is value to the investor to be able to collect rent.

In a hot seller's market, the supply and demand drive up the price of all mobile homes. At the time this book was written, we are in a red-hot seller's market, and supply of homes to buy is extremely low. I've seen the price of mobile homes almost double in the last few years.

I personally do not invest in mobile homes for the purpose of appreciation, but it is a nice bonus when it happens.

So now that I've busted those myths, you'll continue learning how mobile home investments can be lucrative for you.

I believe in abundance and that givers gain. I wrote this book without a filter, describing my rewarding wins and raw losses. And I write with almost two decades of experience in real estate investing. Although I spent eight years in college with only an associate's degree to show, I credit my knowledge to learning outside of formal education. I have spent close to $100,000 on masterminds and coaching outside of traditional education settings.

Now it's your job to take what I give you and put it into practice to build the life of your dreams.

Chapter 1. How and Why I Chose Mobile Homes

I purchased my first site-built home at 20 years old. I had no idea what I was doing, but I had help from a trusted mortgage broker. He guided me to wrap all the closing costs into the loan, which meant I only needed $1,500 out of pocket to say I was a homeowner.

Before that, my friends and I had been evicted for being troubling tenants. As soon as I closed, I told the same friends to move into my house. They each paid me about a third of my mortgage, which meant I lived for free. The downfall is that I learned how our old landlord felt when the place was a mess and the neighbors complained. Yet I felt dealing with that was worth living for free.

A few years later, I called up the mortgage broker to ask if I could buy another house. His reply: "Of course you can!" The price of houses was much higher, but the plan was to refinance in a few years because the market was heading straight up. This was a bad decision. Fast forward a few years, I sold that house as a short sale for less than 50% of what I purchased it for.

That short sale meant banks would not lend me money for 2 years. Once my time in short sale jail was over, I found a house to buy, but then the banks said I had to wait 3 years from the date of my short sale. I didn't want to wait, so I convinced my girlfriend to buy a house. Banks liked her because she had a stable job, paid all her bills on time, and had little debt. I, on the other hand, only worked part of the year and had the short sale on my credit report. We repeated this process a few times and we were making money, but the memories of the short sale grew stronger as housing prices went up. At the time I had no idea this was guiding me towards investing in mobile homes and borrowing money from friends.

Years later an old high school friend sent me a Facebook invite to a monthly meeting. One month I decided to check out this meeting that she was so persistent on inviting me to. It was a Real Estate Investors Association, or REIA, meeting. Everyone in the room made money from real estate or wanted to learn how to make money from real estate. I quickly fell in love with these meetings and went to 3 to 8 a week!

I couldn't get enough of the knowledge or the opportunity to grow my network. Once I became a regular, I realized most of these meetings had a group of guys and girls in the back of the room that had been in the business longer than I had been alive. I started talking to them more, which is when I found the common theme of investing in mobile homes! These experienced investors all owned or had previously owned mobile homes.

At that point in my investing career, I was in the shiny object phase where everything sounded like a great way to invest. My plan was to wholesale properties until I had the cash for a down payment on another house. This meant I needed to do marketing (we'll talk about those strategies in a later chapter). Eventually I received a call from someone needing to sell a mobile home. I walked the mobile home, but my ego said I could never own anything like it.

I reached out to Chris, a fellow investor, and assigned the rights to the contract to him. The 1965 single wide with land was exactly what he was looking for. Chris was not scared of the rats and remodel it needed. I met Chris and the seller at the title company and learned I left one important item out on the agreement—the mobile home! Mobile homes are personal property, and they need to be included on the agreement under personal property. Typically, this is done by the vehicle identification number, but can include a description such as "1965 white single wide." This will tell the title company the mobile home is included in the sale. I followed up with Chris to see how the mobile home investment was going and found out he was receiving more cash flow than he would with a site-built home.

My shiny object syndrome began taking its toll. I became frustrated that I wasn't finding big wholesale deals even though what I really wanted was another rental. But I wasn't finding that either. My mistake was my lack of focus because I was still following the shiny objects in front of me.

One of my favorite real estate meetings is "The Old Jack Miller" meeting. Twice a month, I had dinner at IHOP with about 20 real estate investors who loved to share their stories and experience. An older gentleman with a flea market hat covered in dollar symbols, Andy, talked proudly about the cash flow he received from mobile homes. At that time, Andy was an *ender*, or someone that doesn't need to buy any more properties. Based on their portfolio and success, enders continue in the business of real estate investing because they enjoy it.

Andy approached me to buy a mobile home with the land from him because the tenants were slow at paying him. I door knocked to find out if the tenants were willing to have a conversation, or if they were going to slam the door in my face. Luckily, they were willing to talk. Andy gave me a deal I could not refuse.

By this time, I had purchased a hand full of properties but was still a novice. Andy said we would meet at a Steak-n-Shake to make the transfer. I knew I was supposed to close at a title company, but Andy was the experienced one, so I followed his lead. After our frugal breakfast, I handed Andy a check for $10,000 and he signed a *quitclaim deed* over to me. This is a type of deed that doesn't provide a warranty that the title is clear of liens and encumberments.

I was extremely fortunate that Andy was an honest person, and the quitclaim deed did not cause any major problems. I believe this was the exception to the rule to never buy with a quitclaim deed. The slow-paying tenants continued to have excuses of why they were not paying. I would explain these excuses to my lovely wife, and she helped me realize we needed the income from this mobile home to maintain the home and grow our business. I stepped up and gave the tenants the choice of paying or moving out as I served them with an eviction notice. Within days these tenants found all the money they owed me. This repeated a few more times before they moved out.

In the next chapter, we'll see that I love the cash flow from mobile homes, and the steps I had to take when I was out of money.

Key Takeaways

- Mobile homes are personal property.
- Always meet tenants you will inherit.
- Always close with a title company.
- Networking and building relationships are the best form of marketing.
- Run a business not a charity.
- Have a business partner that complements your weaknesses.
- Mobile homes with land produce more cash flow than site-built homes.

Turn to Chapter 1 in your PDF companion for takeaways and photos. To download go to **Lifestyle-rei.com/free-bonus**

Chapter 2. I'm Keeping This One

After my initial mobile home investment experiences, I was hungry for more mobile homes with land because I saw the cash flow in our bank account. This time my marketing brought me a motivated mobile home seller. The seller told me how he was tired of driving thirty minutes to collect rent at odd hours. On top of that, the neighbors would call and complain about the tenant. He only owned one rental and focused the rest of his time on his successful aerial camera business. My first thought was, *I'm keeping this one.*

Mr. Seller and I met at the property around 9 p.m. so I could meet the tenant and attempt to walk the property. I wasn't able to see much of the mobile home because the resident was a hoarder. I sent my title company the agreement and required the seller to provide the current lease, the assignment of lease, and an estoppel letter.

I wanted the lease in the event I needed to evict the tenant; having the exact agreement on file was good practice. I also like to read leases before closing to ensure I'm comfortable with the terms.

The *assignment of lease* transfers the seller's rights in the lease to me as the buyer. The *estoppel letter* outlines what the resident owns and clarifies agreements that are made outside the lease. You need an estoppel letter to prove any verbal agreements. A verbal agreement to pay $100 extra a month needs to be in the estoppel letter, or the tenant may decide the extra $100 was only intended for the seller. The estoppel may also specify pets and repair agreements that differ from the lease.

The sales price was $15,500, and I was about $15,000 short in my bank account. I knew banks wouldn't finance this mobile home because it was a 1968. But I wasn't going to let my lack of money and the banks' loan reluctance to loan money on a 1968 mobile home stop me from purchasing this cash-flowing mobile home.

I'd heard of "private money" but didn't know how it worked. Come to find out a friend named Kevin wanted to lend some money from his self-directed IRA (SDIRA). This is a perfect example of private money that could help me with this type of investment. I informed the title company so they could prepare the mortgage and note.

Jennifer from the title company met me at the seller's house to sign all the documents. Woohoo! I'd purchased my third mobile home in two months! This time I thought I had done everything right but quickly learned a valuable lesson: I had not asked who provided the water to this home.

The street this mobile home was on used to be a mobile home park until the previous owner subdivided the lots, then individually sold them. What he did not do was get individual wells. He kept one well and charged a monthly fee for use. The monthly water usage fee was not a problem because the owner charged less than the county would have. The issue came in when he would turn the water off without notice, which caused the water heater element to burn up. This meant no hot water for the tenant and a maintenance expense for me.

I decided it was time for me to get serious about my education in real estate investing.

Key Takeaways

- An assignment of lease transfers the interest in the lease from the seller to the buyer.
- Estoppel letters help the new owner to understand who owns what and any agreements that are outside of the lease.
- Review the mobile home leases before closing.
- Borrowing from a friend's SDIRA is a fantastic way to finance mobile homes.
- Ask the seller who supplies the utilities.

Turn to Chapter 2 in your PDF companion for takeaways and photos. To download go to **Lifestyle-rei.com/free-bonus**

Chapter 3. Education

I was making money from real estate after these mobile home investments. My wife and I decided to live off her income as a registered nurse and reinvest all of our profits from our real estate investing. To increase my profitability I recognized the importance of continuing my education, so I started taking all kinds of classes on real estate investing.

I did not take the get-rich-quick overnight TV star classes or the professional realtor classes. I learned from seasoned investors who are currently earning money from their real estate investments. I attended classes on paper-work, options, lending money, SDIRAs, land trusts, deal structuring, how to help sellers, property management, master leasing, subject-to the existing mortgage, and more.

Some classes helped me realize what I definitely want to do, others helped me realize what I do not want to do within the real estate investing world. I also quickly learned one key takeaway from these classes: the power of networking. I started getting to the classes early, finding someone to have lunch with, and staying late. I didn't initially realize the importance of the friendships I was building. Now I can call a friend when I need help putting a puzzle together to help a seller.

I have never been to a class where I didn't learn something. Most of the time, I learned what to do, but the most valuable lessons I have learned are what NOT to do. Some of the best deals are the ones you don't buy!

I also joined a mastermind group and hired a coach. This was harder to do than all the education I pursued. It wasn't because it cost more, but because my ego got in the way. I was afraid of joining a scam and being wrong. I also felt a little ashamed to need a coach because I was admitting I did not know it all. I changed my mind about coaching when I heard a podcast host say, "Michael Jordan had many coaches even when he was at his peak, why do you think you're better than Michael Jordan?"

Hiring a coach and joining a mastermind ended up being some of the best decisions of my life. I do believe I would still be successful without these two decisions, but because of them my growth was accelerated. I cannot imagine my life without a coach or a mastermind. I've built some of the closest bonds and been challenged to stay accountable to my goals, thanks to my mastermind families and coaches.

I know I would not have the life I do today without my education and taking action. This is one reason I am now teaching. I'm doing my part to pass down the knowledge I learned from my teachers and mentors. They taught me through their successes and failures, which is exactly what I do.

To continue your investor education, visit Lifestyle-rei.com This will enable you to make quicker and more confident decisions to increase your cash flow.

Key Takeaways

- Never stop learning.
- Networking at seminars is just as important as learning class content.
- Learn from people that are currently in the business.
- Joining the right mastermind is a very powerful thing.
- A good coach guides you in the right direction.

Don't forget to turn to Chapter 3 in your PDF companion for takeaways and photos. To download go to **Lifestyle-rei.com/free-bonus**

Chapter 4. Subject-to and Affirmation

I finally became an official mobile home investor—not a site-built house investor, not a note investor, not an apartment complex investor, and not a rehab and sell investor. I have declared my niche as buying and renting mobile homes. My marketing began working, which allowed us to wholesale the properties that didn't fit our strict buying criteria.

One of my buying criteria that is often challenged is my buying area—I have to be able to drive to my properties. Sitting in a car and driving all day is not something I'm interested in, so I strictly buy in areas within 30 minutes of my house. I decided from the start to build a business that will give me the life I want.

During an out-of-town visit with Ken, my coach, I got a hot lead. I scheduled the appointment to meet with the seller as soon as I got home. It was a beautiful 1980s single wide on one-and-a-quarter acres.

As the seller was showing me around, I noticed the For Sale By Owner signs sitting inside her house. I asked why they were not in the front yard.

The seller responded, "I bought these six months ago, but I just do not want a bunch of people walking through my house."

Understandable.

We continued talking which was how I found out she was selling to buy a travel trailer and move to the Florida Keys to retire. I got excited for her because I love to travel, and I love seeing people who actually do what they dream of doing.

Eventually, she said, "Why don't you buy the land from me for cash and take over the payments on my mobile home?"

We wrote down our agreement and sent it off to the title company. When we were at the title company to sign the documents, I let her know everything I knew about buying her property subject-to her mortgage. Everything was going great, and I was excited about how I had helped her. This was exciting because I applied my education by purchasing a property in a method I'd learned about.

A month later, I was humbled. The mortgage company refused to talk to me because I was not listed on the mortgage. I had to talk to them because I had updated insurance from a homeowner's policy to a rental policy. I nervously called the previous owner, hoping she had not disappeared on the beach. Thankfully, all my rapport building and genuine caring about her paid off because she filled out the needed power of attorney without hesitating. Relationships matter!

Then the AC wouldn't work. Hmm, this was not good in the Florida heat! The AC company said it was an easy fix—just a broken wire under the home. But then it turned out to be broken in a weird way as if something ripped it off. I found out that the neighbor's goat escaped and happened to go under the home and pulled the wire with his horns. I laughed to myself and realized this was one of many reasons why mobile homes should have skirting.

Skirting should surround the entire home for multiple reasons, and especially because it's a code violation to not have skirting. Skirting helps keep rodents out...as well as goats. It should have vents in it to allow proper airflow under the home. This airflow is important to prevent fungus and mold growth. Professionally installed skirting can easily be removed to perform maintenance or inspection.

When you are buying a mobile home, you want to inspect the tie-downs or straps and the blocks the home sit on. Every municipality has different codes of how far apart these can be, so be sure to do your homework.

Why should you care about the straps and blocks? Because this is how the mobile home is attached to the ground. This is how you prevent it from becoming a hurricane missile. Plus, insurance also cares about this. Owner-occupied insurance requires these straps and blocks to be up to code.

Just a quick note that we use an insurance company that specializes in real estate investors that does not require these to be updated. For more information visit Lifestyle-rei.com/companieswetrust

When I was with my coach, we discussed a plan to replace Erin's income in one year with rental income. We reviewed our current NET rental income, how much we needed to live a good life, and how much an average property produced each month. We decided I needed to buy ten properties to accomplish this goal. That was a stretch goal for me!

I had never purchased ten properties within a year before, but my coach said he believed I could do it if I believed it. When I got home, I purchased a whiteboard and put ten numbered lines on it. At the bottom, I had the total dollar value needed and the total we had.

1. Saddle Bag LN	526.12
2. Kings Manor Lot 2	137
3. Kings Manor Lot 33	273.53
4. Tranquil Acres Lot 40	272.47
5. Daisy	325
6. JA 61	
7. W Chase	409.95
8. Country Club LN	
9.	
10.	
	1933/3000

Next, I used every opportunity to tell Erin I'd have her income replaced by the end of January and she could retire. I know Erin didn't believe this the first few months. Heck, I'm not sure I believed it the first few months.

But as a few properties went on the board and a few hundred dollars each added up, I could see the possibility becoming more feasible. At this time of our lives, Erin and I were frugally living off her income as an RN. This meant we could snowball everything our real estate business produced.

I still remember one of the conversations when I believe Erin had finally gained faith in the plan. We were walking in a beautiful historic city in Europe, admiring a church that was lit up like a castle. Erin and I began to discuss the plan again for what felt like the thousandth time.

We were about two-thirds of the way to accomplishing our financial goal. I reiterated the plan and explained our worst-case scenario. We were set up to have six months of her income in the bank. Stability is important to Erin, so the ability for her to still get a monthly check was important.

I explained that we could put the six months of cash in a separate bank account with biweekly transfers set up. This would feel like she was still getting a check. We never did this, but knowing it was possible built up her confidence in the event the real estate business suddenly died.

A few months later, we had nine mobile homes with land on the board, and the end of January was only a few weeks away! Erin decided to stick to the plan by giving her two weeks' notice even though we were technically one property short.

Luckily, we found that one property quickly, and Erin found a part-time job she enjoyed more. This position meant she was the RN to help when someone was sick or needed time off. She could say no to working if she wanted, and she only had to work one day every three months.

Erin is a fantastic RN who loves helping and caring for people in their time of need, which is why she picked up extra shifts. But our new financial set up gave her the freedom to avoid asking off work if we wanted to go on vacation or go out for a friend's birthday. The employer-employee power had shifted from Erin needing to work to her employer asking her to work.

In hindsight, I realize when I was telling Erin over and over about how I was going to replace her income, I was actually affirming myself to believe it.

Key Takeaways

- Rapport building and genuinely caring pays off.
- It is not the title companies' job to make sure you have all the correct paperwork.
- Mobile home skirting is for more than looks.
- Tie-downs and blocks requirements change depending on the part of the country you live in.
- Whiteboard exercises are visualizations that create momentum.
- What you say daily is a form of affirmation.

Did you do it yet? Turn to Chapter 4 in your PDF companion for takeaways and photos. To download go to **Lifestyle-rei.com/free-bonus**

Chapter 5. Marketing

Growing my real estate business is important to me, which is why I focus a lot of my time on marketing. As I was ramping up my business, I still had more time than money to spend on marketing. I purchased blank yard signs, and Erin used a marker to handwrite Erin Buy$ Mobile Homes. My Friday night job was to put these signs on street corners.

These yielded many calls and leads for years. Without realizing it, I was building brand awareness. People would ask, "Your wife, Erin, is the one with the yellow signs that buys mobile homes, right?"

Disclaimer: Be careful where you put signs because some municipalities have laws against their placement. Check with your local laws to know where you are allowed to place your signs.

We used Erin's name because research shows that women are more appealing for marketing than men. If we were going for the big professional company, we would have done printed signs. But we created handwritten signs because the personality of our brand is "the person next door." We added green highlights to the sign, but not to the essential words because every color but black fades fast when left in the sun. We also added a scribble line on the back to prevent someone from wanting to take the sign and reuse the back.

Location of the signs is important to receive the right calls and to not have code enforcement departments calling you. We chose to put the signs facing those who were leaving neighborhoods we wanted to buy in. Other places where we hoped to catch people's attention included semi-busy stop signs, highway exits, and exits from busy plazas with stores like Walmart, Home Depot, Lowes, grocery stores, and gas stations.

We did not put signs in people's yards, where the grass is overgrown, in spots blocking a driver's view, city or county parks or property, downtown, or an intersection where there were already 3 or more signs. We split our buying area into five sections which allowed us to rotate where we put the signs. This meant an area only had a sign placed in the same locations every five weeks.

Networking

The signs proved helpful, no doubt. But my best lead source is being a human billboard and megaphone. I wear a bright yellow shirt everywhere I go, and I go to a lot of places. My shirt reads "My Wife Buys Mobile Homes," and I tell everyone what we do while giving them a business card. This was meant to be an icebreaker so people would approach me, but it became my brand because people love it.

The first few months of wearing my T-shirt daily did not yield one person's comment or phone call. I now realize this was because I wore the shirt without confidence! Marketing works better when it's backed up with confidence. I attend multiple Real Estate Investor Association (REIA) meetings every week with the purpose of learning and networking. I found the key to networking is to genuinely care what the other person has to say and find a way to help them.

Over months and years, people remember me because I wear the same T-shirt ALL the time. You do not need to look like a yellow highlighter—the key is to find your own way to be memorable.

Our best leads come from other investors and realtors. Most investors don't care about mobile homes. Not all realtors want to spend their time on an agreement that yields so little. Remember that I put in the time to earn these investors and realtors' trust by building rapport. You can too.

Success changes your financial situation. Now I have more money than time for marketing. This means I don't spend my Friday nights driving around town, putting out signs. I still attend many REIA meetings because they are very enjoyable, and I always learn something.

Referrals

Referrals are some of the highest quality leads you can get. The warmer the referral, the better the quality. If I were to rate the quality of a referral, I would put a lunch meeting at the top because there will be a real bond created.

The lowest quality would be sending me an address of a seller that you have never talked to. Some examples of middle quality leads would be a group text or email introduction, or giving a seller my card and letting the seller know I will reach out.

People do business with people they know, like, and trust. When a proper introduction is made, you instantly transfer some trust. I am not a current member of Business Networking International (BNI), but this is the principle behind the business networking group. I love BNI's motto: "Givers gain."

With money, paid marketing can work. The main difference in paid marketing for mobile homes and traditional site-built homes is changing the word *house* to *mo-*

bile home. This means you can still use handwritten yellow letters, postcards, professional letters, door hangers, door knocking, search engine ads, social media ads, print ads, and more.

When I try out a new marketing idea, I commit to experimenting for 6 months. That way I get real feedback from the market to make a decision if the marketing is worth the money and effort. I use a different phone number for each type of marketing, but you don't have to be this complex. You may simply ask each caller how they heard of you.

Yard signs

Yard signs have been a great lead generator. We use yellow with a black handwritten message and green highlights to add color. I suggest you find an easy-to-read combination of colors to stand out.

At our prime of using this marketing, we put out 50 signs each week. We rotated our area where we placed the signs every 5 weeks. These get the phone ringing, but half of our calls these days are spam, people looking to buy a property, or people looking for a rental. In the past, we also received calls from other investors wanting to buy properties from us and contractors looking for work.

If you are handwriting your signs, I recommend a Pilot brand marker because the sun fades them more slowly. If you plan to have these professionally printed, it's possible to send an image of your handwriting. All these options work if you actually do them!

Door knocking

Many of my mentors became known in their neighborhoods by door knocking. This is not as intimidating as it sounds. Door knocking is more than just buying homes—it can be a way of gathering information that doesn't show up on Google.

One afternoon, I was door knocking a neighborhood I thought I wanted to buy within. I was halfway around the circle when I got in a long conversation with some renters. One proceeded to tell me how the cops are there daily, and there's drug use at a few homes. I became a little nervous because my car was parked in the area she referred to. Luckily my car was safe, but I learned I didn't want to own a property in that neighborhood.

When door knocking, I have found it best to go empty-handed. That means no clipboard, no sunglasses, no name tag, etc. I carry a pen and postcards in my pocket. The key is to be approachable. If you wear a smile and a good attitude while asking for help, you'll find people who can help you find motivated sellers in the neighborhood.

Google AdWords

Clicking a button and having the phone ring is my type of marketing because it takes less effort. I have purchased a mobile home from doing Google AdWords, but it can be expensive.

Some large-scale investors spend over $10,000 a month on Google AdWords, which is above my budget. Being in the niche of mobile homes does narrow the competition, and I would imagine being in a small market could improve your chances of success with this method.

I hired someone to place the ads when I was able to purchase. I believe he did a better job because he knows the Google algorithm and reviews the feedback to make adjustments. You can search for your city, and "I buy mobile homes" to see what ads come up. Use these as references when you make your own ads.

Social media

Social media is a huge topic for marketing. I have focused on Facebook because it's the platform I was already using. There are entire books written on the topic of Facebook marketing, so I am going to barely scratch the surface. Within Facebook I advertise on my personal page, in Facebook groups, and on my business page.

On my personal page, I aim for 70% fun. This could be posting photos out with my friends, inspirational quotes, or standing in front of a beautiful waterfall wearing my T-shirt. The rest of the time, I promote my business or ask for referrals. I share my business page posts often.

In Facebook groups, I ask for help and referrals of people needing to sell, contractor recommendations, or I share a useful tip. Think of a Facebook group as a chat room or group setting with a common theme. I am in groups for my local town, national real estate groups, and my individual interests in Jeep or bicycle clubs. Remember that givers gain. Don't bombard any of these groups with your marketing, or you won't get the feedback you wish for.

A business page on Facebook is a long-game marketing strategy. These take months and sometimes years of work to get the slightest traction. I post 5 days a week with the same model of 70% fun. The fun can be silly memes, jokes, or fun facts. The rest of the time I am making posts to ask for mobile homes to buy.

Facebook wants businesses to spend money, so business pages do not get the same exposure as a personal page. It's important to ask people to interact with your page. I ask people to go to posts and to like, comment, and share them.

The time of day you post is very important too. Facebook makes this easy with their option to schedule your posts. If you decide that's too much work, you can always hire a company to do it for you. Like and follow my business page for pro tips and ideas how to market your business: Facebook.com/Lifestylerei.

Paid Facebook ads are cheaper than Google AdWords, and I have found them to be similarly effective. There is a science of which picture to use, how to word the post, and when to run your ads. Again, that can be a part-time job, and I have found better results when I hired a professional to run the ads.

Mailers

There are many types of mailers. Postcards, yellow letters (handwritten notes), and professional letters to name a few. There are many theories of what works best, but I won't go into deep detail about because I'm not an expert.

Most people either do a targeted list of pain points like eviction, divorce, probate, absentee owner, or code enforcement. Recently it has become more popular to mail every door in the neighborhood.

We don't particularly like mailings because the return call rate is very low, and the competition is very high. However, I do have friends that do very well from their mailers. They are very consistent with their mailing cycle and hire someone to make sure it gets done.

Another bonus is that you can print and send mailers from your home. The best mailers are the ones you send!

Print ads

We've had some luck with a print ad in a local coupon book. There are also other options that we have not tried yet such as newspapers, magazines, billboards, and local sponsorships.

Other marketing

I would put my T-shirt in the category of other marketing. It's been fantastic for my business, yet I cannot link one purchase back to the T-shirt. But my T-shirt has made it easy for people to remember me, and it's built credibility in my local community and my real estate investors community.

A T-shirt will not work unless you believe it will. I had zero people approach me the first 3 months of wearing my T-shirt every day. Now multiple people approach me a week. The difference is how I wear the T-shirt. Now I wear it with confidence!

Other marketing ideas that might spark some creativity include: flyers at a laundromat, Koozies, sponsoring community events, partnerships with local businesses, and a sign spinner.

Since writing this book, I've tested more marketing strategies.

Since some of my best deals came from older generations looking to downsize or change living arrangements, I decided to give newspaper ads a try. In my mind, this generation still values getting their news via newspaper. Plus, there's now an online version for digital readers. As you may recall, I needed to commit six months to properly test this marketing strategy. During that time, I didn't get a single appointment from a newspaper ad. Therefore, we decided to cancel this marketing strategy.

Another marketing strategy I've tried is sponsoring local events as well as charity events. I started doing more of this because one of the reasons I desire freedom from financial stress is to have the ability to donate more to charity. I feel fortunate to be able to give back without any expectation of a return. Sometimes, the charity asks to include my business name as a supporter. For me, it's more about giving and doing what I feel is right with my income. You can learn more about some of our favorite charities online at...

www.Lifestyle-rei.com/charity

Last, I have doubled down on networking as my primary marketing strategy because it fits my personality and it's fun. I have found when we keep marketing fun, we actually do it.

Plus, it's more genuine. This is one reason I created a course called, "How to Market Yourself Like a PRO!"

The course is about much more than simply wearing a bright yellow T -shirt everywhere you go. And for those of you who may be introverts...don't worry, I didn't forget about you.

In my experience, when you are the marketing, you don't need a big marketing budget. I've seen investors put such a large portion of their earnings into a marketing budget, but if they only knew how to market themselves like a pro, their marketing budget could easily become their *vacation* budget.

Are you interested in learning how to Market *Yourself* Like a Pro?

For more info, visit...

www.Lifestyle-rei.com/marketyourself

One approach to marketing I've found that has worked extremely well is simply asking for help. Asking for help wasn't always easy for me, but what I've noticed is people are grateful for the opportunity to help the people they know, especially when it involves selling their mobile homes or solving a real estate problem.

During my journey as an educator, as well as an author for this book, I've asked for a lot of feedback on my approach to teaching.

My advice when asking for feedback is to not overthink it; in other words, just ask for what you need.

Here are the phrases I often use to ask for feedback on my book:

"Would you please write a few words of your biggest takeaways from this book on Amazon's website? This will help others know if my book is right for them, and it means a lot to me."

See how easy that is? Of course, modify it as needed to make it your own. Remember that kind words in a referral or a review helps brighten everyone's day.

If I wasn't blunt enough, I'll be looking for your review on Amazon, GoodReads.com, Facebook/Lifestylerei, and other book websites. ☺

Key Takeaways

- Setting yourself apart makes you more memorable.
- Relationship marketing is a long-term game.
- New marketing requires at least 6 months of data to know if it works.
- Consistency and omnipresence are a big part of being memorable.

All right! You know the drill. Turn to Chapter 5 in your PDF companion for takeaways and photos. To download go to **Lifestyle-rei.com/free-bonus**

Chapter 6. The Title and Inspection

On a Wednesday afternoon, I stepped away from a property I was working on to take a phone call. It was a motivated seller responding to one of my yard signs! I sat in my car to cool off while learning about the property.

Their property was a standard 1980 single wide with three bedrooms and two bathrooms on almost a quarter acre lot. The seller told me how he used to rent it, but the people did not take good care of the place, meaning he was a tired landlord. Tired landlords are created by not setting expectations for their tenants and not having systems to set their business up for success.

In my class Full-Time Landlord, Part-Time Work, I teach our system of setting these expectations to keep tenants longer and reduce our management time.

I put work at our current property on pause so I could go look at this new lead. The property was vacant and without power, but I liked what I saw. The seller implied the property was worse than what I observed. I spent time checking for soft spots in the subfloors, especially around the toilets, showers, windows, and doors. I checked the integrity of the windowsills even though there was central air conditioning. I checked because people still tend to leave the windows open or have the window unit air conditioning installed wrong, which leads to water damage. The ceiling was free of water damage. This was especially important to me because roof leaks cause mold damage. This was a rare walkthrough because there were no signs of plumbing leaks under the sinks.

During my walkthrough, I saw the original interior wallboard and located the data plate in the master bedroom closet. The *data plate* includes the VIN, year of the home, wind zone rating, and more. This is not a must-have, but it is helpful to know what you're buying.

On June 15, 1976, the Department of Housing and Urban Development (HUD) required that manufacturers place this large information sticker, or data plate, on the interior of every mobile home manufactured. I have only seen this in the master bedroom closet and inside of the breaker box door, but I have read about it being located inside a kitchen cabinet door at times. It's good practice to match the VIN from the data plate with the VIN on the title of the home(s) to ensure you are purchasing the correct home.

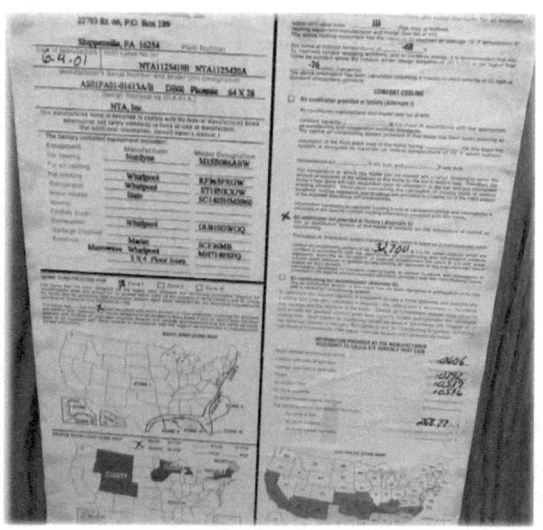

It's not uncommon that the data plate has been removed when remodeling, or sometimes the home is so old that it never had one. In this case, if the home still has a tongue (or the hitch) that the home was originally pulled with, there should be a VIN on it. Most of the tongues have been removed and sold for scrap metal. If this is the case, you will need to crawl under the home with a flashlight and search the forward cross-member of the steel I-beam frame. HUD required that a VIN was stamped into the metal which had a minimum height of 3/8 inch.

A single wide has one VIN/title, a double wide has two VINs/titles, and a triple wide has three VINs/titles. The VIN should be the same number on all the titles for the double- and triple wide except for one letter. A double wide will have an A side and a B side. A triple wide will have an A side, B side, and C side. This means the mobile homes were meant to be married together. Mobile home title(s) look like the title of your car or truck.

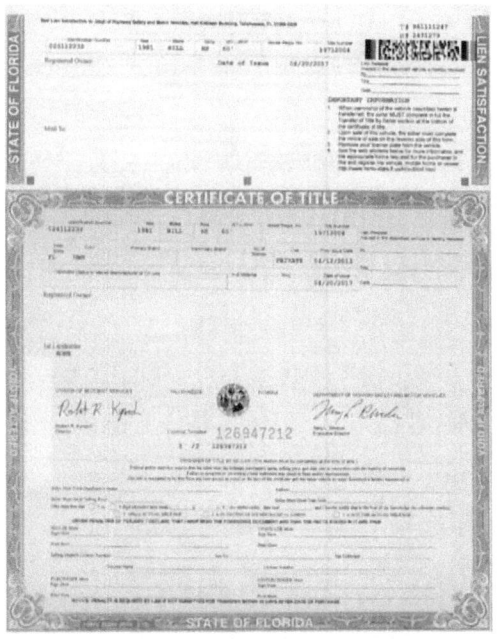

Back to my conversation with Mr. Seller. Once I called him back, we spent some time talking about price. We came to an agreement pending an inspection with power on. I wanted the power on so I could check the electrical and central AC system. Even though the sellers were local, we did everything over the phone by their choice.

Banks do not like to finance 1980s mobile homes for investment purposes. During my conversation with the seller, the idea of making payments came up, but it didn't work for his goals. This left me two options—spend my own cash, or offer the opportunity for a friend to lend me the money.

For that mobile home, I gave a friend the opportunity to finance it. I knew she had some money sitting in her SDIRA waiting to make a return. A self-directed IRA, or SDIRA, allow us to invest in real estate. There are few rules and fees involved.

There are many custodians who offer free training to make sure you comply with the laws. These are powerful because our friend made a higher return than a standard stock dividend, while having security on an asset managed by a trusted friend versus a large company managed by people the friend doesn't know. I love using private money to fund our purchases because I can have a conversation with my friend about the terms of the loan.

A few weeks later, I met a mobile closing notary at a McDonald's and signed all of my paperwork, including the transfer of the mobile home title. As much as I love meeting the sellers, not everyone wants to meet in person to sell their mobile home. We must conform to the seller's needs to help ease them through this transition in their life.

Key Takeaways

- Soft spots in the subfloor are common around the toilet, shower, windows, and doors.
- Windowsills commonly rot from improperly installed window AC units, or from the windows being left open.
- Mobile homes made from June 15th, 1976, or later have a data plate in the master bedroom closet, electric panel door, or inside a kitchen cabinet door.
- Banks do not like to finance older mobile homes, but friends with SDIRAs can lend you the money.

You know what I'm going to say...Turn to Chapter 6 in your PDF companion for takeaways and photos. To download go to **Lifestyle-rei.com/free-bonus**

Chapter 7. Moving a Mobile Home

My uncle called me about his friend Joe who needed to sell his mobile home with an acre of land. I got excited because it was my ideal property—a 1980s double wide with 3 bedroom and 2 bathrooms. It was a beautiful, desirable neighborhood, and it had a fenced backyard, a screened porch, and a few sheds.

I met Joe at the property, and we discussed his situation of having two homes but only being able to live in one. The mobile home didn't need much work to have it in rent-ready condition, so I got even more excited. We agreed upon a price, but then Joe and his wife decided they weren't going to sell.

Joe and his wife had new plans where they were going to sell the current mobile home and put a new one on the lot. He asked me how much we would pay for only the home. After searching my contacts, I found an investor with a vacant lot needing a mobile home. What a perfect match!

I met Joe to exchange the title and money. Then I was the owner of the double wide! I met with Mr. Buyer to sign an agreement and collect money from him. I made a profit and technically was done, but Mr. Buyer had never moved a mobile home before. The process took much longer than anyone expected, so I had to play the peacemaker.

Joe wanted the mobile home off his property. The movers allegedly damaged Joe's property, and the inspectors from the county took longer than anyone thought. Thankfully by the end of the month, the mobile home was moved to Mr. Buyer's land, and Joe was happy he had a vacant acre to put a new home on.

This was an important transaction for me because I learned buying and selling mobile homes to be moved is not my area of expertise. This was a wonderful reminder that my life is better when I focus on what I am best at and what makes me the most money. My niche is a single unit mobile home with the land! However, I do want to have a solution for every person that contacts us with a troubling situation.

I met an investor named Rod while networking. He is a licensed dealer. Rod's business is buying and selling used mobile homes which need to be moved. Rod and I discussed how we could work together. We determined that I would send him prescreened motivated leads and a check would show up for me. This enables us to help people in need, make some money, and stick to our investing niches.

Key Takeaways

- You learn from every deal.
- The riches are in the niches.
- Utilize other people's time/expertise.

Let's say it together now...Turn to Chapter 7 in your PDF companion for takeaways and photos. To download go to **Lifestyle-rei.com/free-bonus**

Chapter 8. An Accidental Fix-and-flip

Greed is something people may encounter on their way to success. It can help us become super performers in business, but it can also get us into trouble by making us act outside of our business vision.

I decided early on that we weren't going to buy and rent properties in rough areas. I consider a rough area as one where the cops show up on a regular basis, where there are more wooden windows than glass, and where I do not feel safe. Greed convinced me to break this rule one time.

The projected numbers of one mobile home investment looked so enticing that I told myself it would be worth the hassle for the extra income. *Plus, this mobile home was on County Club Lane. What a beautiful sounding road.*

Wrong!

This double wide had two bedrooms but used to have three, and I knew we could easily put the wall back up. There were two bathrooms with only a little subfloor damage in one from the sliding glass door. This was a quick and easy project, and my handyman agreed. I sat down with the owner's daughters because the owner's dementia had progressed to the point where she could no longer legally make the decision to sell.

I sent the details to one of my private money lenders. He was thrilled about the ROI. The title company requested that a doctor submit a letter stating that the owner didn't have the mental capacity to make the decision to sell. This gave the daughters the power of attorney to sign for their mom.

My handyman started working on the scope of work the day we closed. He had everything done in about a week, which meant we could put up the For Rent sign. I was showing the property more than normal but without applications returned. The advertised rent price was $700, which I felt was fair, yet the lack of applications made me second guess my decision.

As I was showing the home, I asked people what they could pay or what they were paying now. Their replies were closer to $400, which shocked and worried me.

I received a reply to a Craigslist ad from what I judged to be a wholesaler, so I blew him off. He kept messaging me, so I finally said, "I will be there at 1 p.m. to show the place to a few people." He showed up, walked the home, and said he was interested in paying cash for it.

My wholesaler radar went off, and I told him to send me an offer. I went back to my prospective rental applicants, but no luck. Within a few hours, I had an all-cash offer from the investor, which was a little low. This was a perfect opportunity to sharpen my negotiating skills. I didn't meet him in the middle. I only budged a tiny bit on price, which was enough for him. We had an agreement.

By then, I was more excited about selling for cash than I was about the monthly income the mobile home could produce because I ultimately didn't feel safe with the property. Within a week I saw the SWAT team raiding a house in the neighborhood. The small garden gate to the property was stolen. And I knew Erin would never feel safe going to this property.

Mr. Buyer was from out of the country, with cash to spend and a flight back. He was a motivated buyer with cash. My private money agreement stated I had a 10% penalty for paying the loan back before four years. I let him know I was paying the 10% penalty plus a little extra because I made a profit. We closed on the last business day of the year. This was my first fix-and-flip, and I received a nice check for it. I was very fortunate to make money on a learning experience like this.

I learned a few great lessons on this accidental fix-and-flip: I need to stick to my ideal neighborhoods! Negotiating is easier when the other party is more motivated than you. Finally, always take extra good care of your private money lenders. This was better than a seminar because I got paid!

I did follow this property on Zillow for the next year, and it went up for rent three times. I became even more grateful that I'd sold it. My vision of my business does not include setting myself up for work—renting the same property three times a year sounds like a lot of effort to me.

Key Takeaways

- Do not buy in areas you do not feel safe in.
- Doctors can document medical conditions to enact a power of attorney and empower the assigned parties to sign closing documents.
- The least motivated individual does the best in a negotiation.
- Always take extra good care of private money lenders when the situation changes.
- Every investor has a different ROI they desire.

Okay. What are we going to do? We're going to turn to Chapter 8 in our PDF companion for takeaways and photos. To download go to **Lifestyle-rei.com/free-bonus**

Chapter 9. People Sell for Other Reasons than Money

Ring! Ring! Another call from our signs on the side of the road.

Frank told me he needed to sell his double wide mobile home with land *now*, so I dashed over. He showed me around, pointing out that the roof was only a few years old, and the central air conditioner was practically new. As I sat on the couch speaking with Frank and his wife, I found out why they need to move so fast—Frank's wife was having health issues.

These challenges were making it difficult for Frank and his wife to keep up with the cleaning and maintenance of the four-bedroom, two-bathroom home. They already found a smaller place in a 55+ neighborhood. One reason they wanted to move into a new community was because the community oversees the outside maintenance. They voiced their concern about what to do with their excess belongings. I informed them to leave anything they did not want, and I would donate what I could.

Frank asked for a fair price, so we signed the agreement. I dropped the signed agreement with a deposit off at the title company on my way home. Two weeks later, we were at the title company when Frank said, "You know you are getting a fantastic deal, right?"

Before I could reply, his wife said, "So are we because we are able to move so fast and focus on my health."

This property could have been sold on the MLS by a realtor for more money, but money is not always the motivating factor for people. This time, a fast closing was more important than money. I had taken time to sit down with Frank and his wife, learning about *why* they needed to sell, then I gave solutions to each challenge.

I decided to pay cash for the property because we had it available, and the cash-on-cash return was so high. I did not ask Frank to lower his price because the property was in great condition and the projected ROI was more important. "Don't steal in slow motion" is something Jack Miller, a renown real estate investor, used to say.

Miller meant that if something is a great deal, don't try to beat the person down to save a few dollars and risk losing the deal. I also knew after I closed, I could call a friend and offer them an opportunity to lend on this free and clear property.

I sleep better at night knowing I have some debt-free properties, which keep my debt-to-income ratio where I feel comfortable. A free and clear property leaves me with the option to borrow cash from a friend quickly if needed.

All we had to do to make the mobile home rent-ready was bring a few truckloads to Goodwill and to the dump. As housing providers, we found a great family to move in; they have been there without an issue for years.

Key Takeaways

- Ask questions to find a person's *why*.
- Solve the problems of *why* a person needs to sell.
- Money is not always a seller's motivating factor.

All right! Chapter 9. PDF companion. To download go to **Lifestyle-rei.com/free-bonus**

Chapter 10. Do Not Get Lazy

Cash flow from mobile home rentals allows me the freedom to travel often. One day while I was waiting to board a flight, I saw an interesting mobile home lead from a wholesaler. We exchanged emails that answered all my questions, and I gave the wholesaler my price range for purchasing.

A few days later, the wholesaler asked me to walk the property, which I knew meant he would accept my price. On my way home from the airport, I stopped to view the property and didn't find anything to scare me off. We signed the agreement, but because he controlled the contract, we were using his title company.

I had confidently purchased many homes by then. And that's when life found a way to humble me. Things had become routine when I bought a mobile home. I sent the title company my closing directions. I sent the lending opportunity to some friends who had told me that they had money. Then I was off hunting for another property.

Closing day arrived, and I stopped by the property for a pre-closing walkthrough and found the backyard fence was broken. It looked like someone tied the fence to a truck and floored it. I called Mr. Wholesaler to inform him we had a problem. I felt it was fair to be compensated for the broken fence; I didn't have this repair in my budget when I made my offer. We came to a fair agreement to split the cost of the fence.

At the closing, I chatted with the friendly title lady, but did not read the documents as closely as I should have. I became a little lazy and assumed everything would go according to my directions. Later I realized some things were done in a different manner than my directions had indicated. Nothing super serious, but it taught me a very important lesson: I now require all title paperwork to be done three business days prior to closing so my title company can review it.

I met my handyman at the property to sign our agreement so he could start swinging a hammer. A few days into rehab, he told me he thought the place had live termites! Having never dealt with termites, this scared me, and I frantically called termite companies. I finally found one that could tent the double wide within two weeks. The termite company recommended bringing any wood we planned to use inside for the fumigation. This ensured we did not bring termites back in. Fortunately, we caught this before we had major damage.

In our contractor agreements, I give a daily bonus for finishing early and a daily penalty for finishing late. Soon after the fumigation, my handyman got sick but remembered the bonus clause in our agreement if he finished the work early. In the past, the job would have completely stopped. But thankfully that clause gave him a reason to get people at the property to finish the work.

As if there were not enough obstacles already, the insurance company notified me that they needed the mobile homes VINs (which they'd never asked for in the past). I knew my purchase did not include the titles for the home, and I didn't care about it because I had received a proper discount. There was no sign of a VIN anywhere. I even offered my handyman $500 if he could find it on the I-beam under the home. Nothing!

Then my lovely wife pointed out the obvious different windows on the two sides of the home. Erin smiled as she asked, "Is this double wide actually two single wide?" *Wow, that is exactly what happened here.*

Whoever married the two single wide homes together did a great job besides the front windows. The only reason I cared was due to the additional insurance costs because it didn't have a VIN.

Even though I hadn't checked for the VIN beforehand, the great news was that the extra expense for insurance didn't make this a negative-cash-flowing property! You always need wiggle room for things you can't foresee happening.

Once I had a tenant moved in, I called the main DMV office asking for help with a new VIN. A lady from the DMV inspected the home for the VIN. She was unsuccessful in locating it and wrote an affidavit stating that. This affidavit included her description of the home, along with my next steps in the process.

Just before filing the final paperwork to set a court date for a new VIN, I found my insurance dropped the rate. I made the decision to call off the quest for a new VIN. Insurance companies are important members of your team! We have multiple agents that we do business with depending on the situation. For more information on the company that saved us, go to Lifestyle-rei.com/companieswetrust_

I had taken action and made a mistake. Luckily, I still made money. The initial mistake may have been a result of laziness, but I learn from each mistake. I now have more lead time on the paperwork, and I always account for something that could go wrong.

Key Takeaways

- Always inspect the property on the day of closing.
- Double check all documents, especially when using a new title company.
- Ask your title company to review closing documents when using a new-to-you title company.
- If you tent a house for termites, put all the wood for the project inside the home to ensure you don't bring in new termites.
- Give your handyman an incentive to finish jobs on time.
- There is an involved process to receive a new VIN.
- Having the right insurance company on your team can save you a lot of money.
- Visit Lifestyle-rei.com/companieswetrust for our preferred insurance company.
- Learn from each mistake.

Takeaways and photos. To download go to
Lifestyle-rei.com/free-bonus

Chapter 11. A Realtor Referral

During a break at a mastermind retreat, I received a message from a realtor. I had met her husband at a networking group I was a part of. Ms. Realtor explained to me she had a client who needed to sell her older single wide. Ms. Realtor didn't want to represent the seller: "I do not want to do the paperwork for a $20,000 mobile home, but I want to help the seller." With a smile, I replied, "I promise to take great care of her, as I do with everyone."

Rudi, the seller, and I talked on the phone about her situation. She was getting married and didn't need this second home. She'd moved almost two hours away about a year prior. She explained that she had the single wide moved to the property a few years prior. I instantly knew the tie-downs and piers were up to code, with a good chance that the home was in great condition. It needed to be roadworthy at the time of the move. I also knew this property was no longer financeable by a bank. Banks do not like to finance a mobile home that was moved from its original installation.

Before we could set up a date to inspect the property, Rudi emailed me pictures. Once I was back in town, Rudi and I met at the single wide. I told her I liked what I saw, and I would put it in writing at her $20,000 asking price. Then Rudi mentioned she had another offer for a little more money.

Before I could reply, she muttered, "I would rather sell to you because the other guy was not as kind as you."

She helped me understand that she needed the extra money for her wedding. Rudi declared she would leave the home "broom-swept clean" if it would help me out. I noted the plumbing and tie-downs both had been recently updated. And Rudi and I came to the agreement that I would match the other offer.

Rudi was able to secure the money from the sale in less than two weeks. This enabled her to afford the wedding of her dreams. The cash to purchase this property was in my bank account, but I decided to use funds from a private money lender. I made this decision to grow our business with sufficient reserves. I had very little work to complete before finding the perfect resident.

I knew we had the perfect resident when the first improvement they did was add colorful plants all around the home. One of the times I stopped to comment on how beautiful the property looked; I was invited in so she could show off the inside. This was the moment I realized there was something special going on because residents like this are key to my business.

I reflected on what went right to attract such a wonderful resident. I remembered that the prospective resident had great communication during the application process, didn't have any issues returning all the requested documents, asked questions about making the home their own, and asked questions about me. This showed me they were not desperate to move nor did they want a short-term lease. Their application backed this up. And this all started with a referral from networking efforts.

Key Takeaways

- Networking continues to be a fantastic lead source.
- Being the nice person pays off.
- Finding the right resident will make your business more profitable.

Okay. Let's all turn to Chapter 11 in the PDF companion for takeaways and photos. To download go to **Lifestyle-rei.com/free-bonus**

Chapter 12. Master Lease

Always leave an offer! One day I door knocked properties that I'd sent email offers to but hadn't received replies from. One property of interest was vacant. I have a rule that if I drive to a property, I leave an offer. I left the offer on the door and forgot about it.

A few months later a sweet lady called me asking if I was still interested. She explained how she sold the property but could not close because of the title work. She showed me around the well-kept property and explained how she'd ended up in her situation.

I stated that I would like to rent the property from her. She lived too far away to be a landlord and didn't want the responsibility. I continued to explain that she would give me the right to sublet it out. This is called a *master lease*. We talked for about an hour longer. She felt comfortable with her options. She was interested, but I told her to think it over and call me the next day. She called me that night, asking when we could meet to sign the lease.

A month into our relationship, her husband whispered to me, "If you can find a way to fix this title work, the property is yours." That meant I'd built enough rapport that they'd allow me to buy the property when I cleared the title.

Investing is about relationships and helping people. Three years earlier, I had attended a multiday seminar about master leasing. I opened my book to refresh myself because this would be my first master lease.

At times I learn a new tool years before I have the chance to use it in the real world. I'm grateful I had the knowledge of master leasing available when the right opportunity presented itself.

Key Takeaways

- Always leave an offer when talking to a seller or stopping at a property.
- Real estate investing is a business built on relationships.
- Opportunities to use real estate education can take time.

You know what's coming. Turn to Chapter 12 in your PDF companion for takeaways and photos. To download go to **Lifestyle-rei.com/free-bonus**

Chapter 13. Repairs

Mobile home repairs will vary depending on the age of the home and if it has been remodeled. One reason mobile homes are built in a factory and shipped to their destination is to provide housing at a very low price. That means that inexpensive materials are often used.

An example is that a 1960s home has very thin walls, to the point you can hear everything in the next room. In June of 1976, the government stated there was a standard that needed to be followed. As of 2004, the same quality materials that are used as in a site-built home are used in mobile homes.

This chapter focuses on some major differences and possible upgrades to your investment.

Roof

There are many different types of roofs for mobile homes. The roof is one of the most important elements of the home to protect your investment. Preventing a roof leak protects against mold growth and other damage.

Prior to the 1976 HUD guideline changes, the roof trusses were all over the map, but often 2" x 2" or 2" x 3" trusses were used. In the post-1976 HUD guidelines, 2" x 4" trusses were typically used, but some builders use 2" x 6"trusses on certain models.

Many newer mobile homes have asphalt shingles like a site-built home. Unlike a site-built home, it is not recommended to have more than one layer of shingles on a mobile home. If you have an older mobile home, you want to be careful with putting asphalt shingles on your roof because the trusses were not built to withstand the weight.

Single-ply membrane roofing is a material that is flexible and easy to install. This is what you see on top of many commercial buildings. Next time you are on a plane, look at the roofs of a big box store and you'll almost be blinded by the bright white roof. These are commonly called *TPO roofs*, which can add to your energy efficiency because the white reflects the sun's heat. A TPO roof is lightweight, which makes it great for all ages of mobile homes. In most cases, TPO can be installed right over an existing roof. This saves you the labor costs of removing the old roof.

These roofs are easy to maintain or repair in a small area. We like to use a product called *Kool Seal*. This is sold at the big box stores and comes in white or black. The white helps reflect the heat, but our northern friends sometimes like the black to retain the heat in the cold months. Kool Seal can easily be rolled on with a paint roller. When we use Kool Seal, we clean the roof and let the roof fully dry before applying it.

Metal roofs are a popular upgrade. I usually see these used as a *roof-over*, which means the metal roof literally sits on top of the existing roof. The sub-roof does need to be in a strong condition to screw the metal roof into. Metal roofs are lightweight, meaning that they can be put over a roof regardless of age. These are great upgrades for additions because one panel of metal running from the center to the end of the addition makes it less prone to leaks.

You could also build a roof-over structure on your mobile home. When people do this, they have posts in the ground to take the weight off the home.

Plumbing

Plumbing materials for mobile homes have changed over the years to be more similar to those found in site-built homes. In the 1980s, it was popular for the manufacturers to use gray PEX piping. The joints of this piping have a very high failure rate. I recommend looking under the home for gray PEX, especially under the sinks.

Installing new plumbing in mobile homes is usually affordable. The crawl space allows easy access, and many mobile homes are built with water lines running in an efficient layout. The layout usually includes laundry on one side of a wall and a sink on the other. The water heater is usually located very close to the bathroom. Typically, the length of total water lines in a mobile home is less than a site-built home with equal square footage.

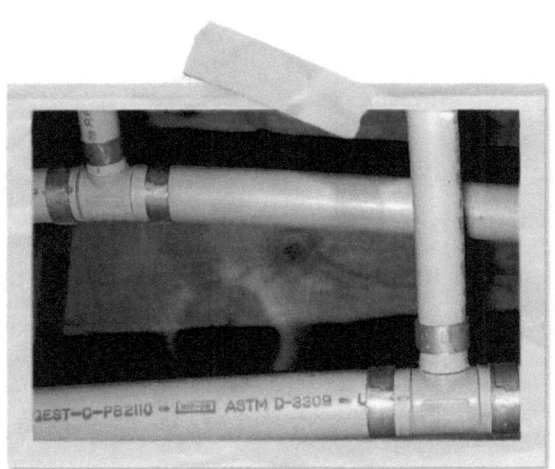

Sewer lines are similar to those in a wood frame house because of the crawl space. If we have an issue with a mobile home, we upgrade from the black piping to PVC. You want to make sure to use a professional plumber because there is a right and wrong way to put together sewer lines.

Some issues I've seen are improper slope and sharp turns of piping, which do not allow the sewage to drain properly.

Electrical

Mobile homes have the main breaker box on a pole independent of the home. Be careful opening the boxes because wasps love to build nests inside the lid. Like site-built homes, aluminum wiring was often used until they realized it was dangerous.

I like to check light switches, look for burn marks on outlets, and look at the breaker box. Rats love to chew electrical wire, so if you see signs of rats, check the electrical system more closely.

My electrician says rewiring a mobile home is not very difficult if it's clean under the home.

90

Here are some unsafe electrical panels to watch for:

- Zinsco (GTE-Sylvania) 1970s
- Federal Pacific Electric (FPE) 1950s–1980s
- Challenger (Eaton/Cutler Hammer) 1980s–1990s

Pushmatic 1950–1980 is not necessarily unsafe, but it is difficult to find parts because the company went out of business.

Subfloors

Pressed particle board was used for many years as the sub-floor for mobile homes. The quickest way to find out if you have particleboard subfloors is to look from the underside (assuming your vapor barrier is not in place).

Replacing subfloors with three-quarter-inch plywood is not difficult. Like a wood frame home, there are beams to attach your subfloor. These beams rest on the metal frame of the mobile home. I have found it common for people to replace small sections of bad subfloors with different thicknesses of wood. It's recommended to replace the entire room to ensure you have a safe home.

Walls

Not all mobile home walls are equal. Before June of 1976 (when HUD came out with standards for mobile homes), the exterior walls were 2" x 2" or 2" x 3" thick and generally had a stud spacing of 16" on center. Interior walls were most commonly 2" x 2" with studs that were 1" x 2" with a 24" stud spacing on center. These thinner walls and doors require a lockset specific to mobile homes.

After June of 1976, exterior walls are 2" x 4" or 2" x 6" and 16" spacing on center. Interior walls are 2" x 3" or 2"x 4".

Most mobile homes have wallboard; it's cheaper and quicker to install than drywall. There are some attractive patterns, but you may find it difficult to replace with a matching color if only one panel needs to be replaced. You can paint wallboard, but you should use oil-based paint. Latex paint can make wallboard peel and bubble.

You can upgrade the studs in a mobile home, as well as upgrade from wallboard to drywall. Upgrading the studs allows you to use a regular house door and lockset.

Belly wrap

When a mobile home is moved from the factory, it appears to be plastic wrapped on the underside. This is called bottom board, belly board, or *belly wrap*. The purpose of this plastic wrap is to keep moisture, insects, and rodents out of the home.

A big sag in the bell wrap is a sign of a water leak. Like subfloor replacement, you'll want to replace the entire area if it is severely damaged. At times you can still do a proper repair if there is only a small tear in the plastic.

Skirting

Skirting comes in different materials such as cement blocks, wood, aluminum, and fiberglass panels. You will commonly find mobile homes that have missing or damaged skirting. This is a major problem because the purpose of skirting is to protect under the home.

This important aspect of mobile homes helps prevent potentially more serious repairs under the home. Correctly installed skirting also keeps out moisture and animals. It also keeps the code enforcement off your back. You do not want to seal under the home with plywood because that prevents airflow.

Supplies for mobile home repairs

Mobile home–specific parts can be purchased at mobile home supply stores. You will commonly find these stores in areas where there are many mobile homes. A quick Google search will help you locate the stores. The big box stores will carry some of these parts as well if there is demand. Within 20 minutes of where I live, one big box store carries mobile home–specific door handles and the other does not. Check with each store.

Water under the home

Water under the home can cause many problems. You need to determine where the water is coming from. Is it poorly placed roof downspouts? Improper grading under the home? Improper lot grading around the home? A broken pipe?

To fix these issues, you need to drain the water and let it completely air out. Then make the appropriate repair.

Mold and structural issues are the main reasons you need to immediately take care of water under a home. Sitting water under the wood floors is a recipe for mold growth, especially in hot months. Standing water softens the ground under the foundation, which could lead to the foundation shifting. An unlevel foundation can lead to cracking in the walls, squeaking floors, and roof separation.

Additions to mobile homes

The laws regarding mobile home additions will be determined by your local municipality. You want attachments to stand alone so they don't weaken the mobile home's ability to stay on the ground during high winds. You need to check with the local building codes to ensure the mobile home has a safe structure.

A few things to consider when adding on to a mobile home are to have two exits, natural lighting, and a crawlspace, and to ensure the electrical system can handle the addition. Sometimes the HVAC system might need to be upgraded too. And finally, consider how an addition would affect the ability to move the home in the future.

Finding the right contractor is key to keeping repair or remodel expenses down and the home safe. When I see someone working on a property, I stop and talk with them to see their work and get their info. I also like running Craigslist ads and asking mobile home park managers who they use.

I choose a contractor based on price, quality, safety, speed, and the amount of time I believe I will have to babysit them. Your contractor is a very important part of your team, so pay them in a timely manner.

Because this chapter is so data heavy, if you're someone with a visual or hands-on learning style, you may have found this chapter challenging. That's why I created courses - so there are pictures, videos, and stories to explain the inspection and repair processes better than words can. You can find a complimentary sample at **Lifestyle-rei.com/free-bonus**

By now you should know...Turn to Chapter 13 in your PDF companion for takeaways and photos. To download go to **Lifestyle-rei.com/free-bonus**

Chapter 14. Why Would You Sell a Nice House Like This?

In the spring of 2019, our portfolio only contained 2 site-built homes, with one on the market. Our residents in that house had decided they needed to downsize because they had become empty nesters.

When we'd purchased that house, the plan was to keep it forever as a rental. But then some educational classes challenged my way of thinking, and I adjusted our original plans. I compared the ROI as a rental to selling the house and using the profit to buy mobile homes. I decided to accelerate our growth by doing this as a 1031 exchange.

A *1031 exchange* is a way to defer your taxes by selling property and putting the gains towards like-kind property without paying the taxes in the year of the sale. The name 1031 exchange comes from the IRS Code Section 1031. It means thousands of dollars are going to work for you right now, which allows you to compound faster before paying taxes.

If you have debt, you also must have the same amount of debt with the new purchase(s). You must identify your new purchase(s) within 45 days of the sale of the property. A new clock starts with 180 days to close on the new property or properties. This is handled by a 1031 exchange intermediary, which for a small fee, helps you follow the law and walks you through the process legally.

I projected the need to purchase 6 individual mobile homes with land. We also decided to take a little of the cash out of the sale to spend. Remember—we believe in enjoying the fruits of our business as we go because that's what life is all about! The 1031 exchange made 2019 my biggest buying year to that point. To accomplish all of this, I increased my marketing budget.

While the house we were selling was being rehabbed, I started my marketing. Over the next few months I did it all: direct mail, Google AdWords, Facebook Ads, reviewing Zillow and the MLS, and most importantly, I let everyone know what I was looking for. My goal was to let everyone know we were buying more mobile homes. Read on for more details about a few of the mobile home transactions I pursued to complete the 1031 exchange.

Key Takeaways

- Evaluate the current performance of your properties every year or two.
- A 1031 exchange can accelerate your growth by deferring paying taxes on profits.
- Start looking for your replacement property (or properties) before you are ready to close on what you are selling.

I feel like we should have the hang of this by now. Turn to Chapter 14. **Lifestyle-rei.com/free-bonus**

Chapter 15. 1031 Exchange Purchase #1

I was off to a fantastic start in the 1031 exchange because Erin found a nice-looking mobile home on Zillow before we sold the house we were exchanging. Erin and I went to the seller's home together. Although I did most of the talking, the seller's wife talked to Erin more. I was the point of contact for the rest of the transaction even though the wife always said, "Tell Erin..." I don't believe we would have purchased this mobile home without Erin's influence.

The challenge with this situation was that the mobile home sellers needed money for their move before I sold the property I was exchanging. I reached out for help from other investors and the 1031 exchange intermediary on how to structure this deal. The solution was to rent the home from the sellers with an option to buy it until I was able to close. This allowed the sellers to get enough cash to move to Colorado while I was still able to purchase the property as part of the exchange.

This little two-bedroom, one-bathroom mobile home had been completely remodeled. It was built in the 1970s, but all the walls were now drywall with a beautiful knock-down finish, newer kitchen cabinets, tile shower walls, and a regular house front door. Some people think you cannot rebuild these older homes. But that's not true. Like any home when it is properly taken care of, it will last.

Another important upgrade made to this home was a metal roof over the original roof. This ensured water would not find its way inside. A leaking roof can quickly destroy an old mobile home.

A few other key features of this property that were particularly attractive were its location on a quiet street with very little traffic, the shed in the backyard, and little work needed to make the home rent-ready.

Key Takeaways

- Sometimes women are more comfortable conducting business transactions with another woman.
- Reach out for help with deal structuring.
- Deals are right in front of you if you have a conversation to solve the seller's problem.

You know what's coming. Turn to Chapter 15 in your PDF companion for takeaways and photos. To download go to **Lifestyle-rei.com/free-bonus**

Chapter 16. 1031 Exchange Purchase #3

A nice lady called the number from one of our yard signs. She stated that she needed to sell fast due to her foreclosure. Of course, I scheduled an appointment for the next morning.

I couldn't start my walkthrough until the owners secured their aggressive dog. But then I walked the property and danced around many holes in the floors. After viewing the entire 1980s single wide mobile home, I sat down with Ms. Seller and her boyfriend. They explained their problems and needs. She came clean about her criminal history, their need for money, the foreclosure, and wanting to move so her adult son took some responsibilities of his own.

As I pointed to the For Sale By Owner sign in the front yard, I asked, "Why haven't you sold it yourself?" Apparently, she had people cancel their contracts because of financing issues. The age and condition of the home had limited the potential buyers' financing options. I gave her two offers—a lower cash price that I could pay in full, or the asking price if she would accept payments.

She was more interested in the asking price, but she needed this foreclosure to stop now. We came to an agreement that I would give her half down to handle the foreclosure as well as some cash to move. This was a bigger rehab project than I typically enjoy, but my estimates determined we would still make money.

We enjoy the win-win situation when we can make a profit and the seller is able to walk away with money versus losing their house to foreclosure.

Similar to exchange purchase #1, I loved that this one was on a quiet street with low traffic, had a large workshop, and had a fenced backyard. These features are great because my avatar resident wants a workshop with a fenced yard.

Key Takeaways

- Give sellers different offers to choose from.
- Solving the seller's problem is part of the value in your offer.

Do I really need to say it? Chapter 16.

To download go to **Lifestyle-rei.com/free-bonus**

Chapter 17. 1031 Exchange Purchase #5

Our My Wife Buys Facebook business page received a message from a guy needing to sell his single wide mobile home. The address and information sounded familiar to me. I searched through our lead records for the address. I had, in fact, talked to the family needing to sell twice before.

The first time we'd talked was from a letter I sent years ago. I walked the home at that time, but they did not like my offer. The second time was a few years later when they replied from an ad posted through Google AdWords. I did not go to the property that time, and instead questioned the owner about changes to the property. Based on the new information, I updated my offer. My cash offer was reject-

ed. The young couple did not want to accept payments because they had debt they wanted to pay off before moving.

The old saying that "the third time is the charm" came
true. This time the husband contacted me because a mutual friend referred him to me. It had only been a few months
since I'd spoken to his wife. I informed him that I needed
an update on the current situation and condition, but my
offers weren't going to change much.

To my surprise, he answered with a date and time to walk
the property with him. While we were walking the property,
I met the current tenants. The seller and I both realized the
single wide was not in as good of condition as we expected.

The owner did not want to spook the tenants about
selling, so we met down the street to talk. He realized the
condition of the property was worse than he'd led me to
believe. He was not lying to me; he just didn't know. He was
a tired landlord. We agreed on a cash price and signed the
agreement on the trunk of my car.

I reminded him that I needed a copy of the current
lease and an estoppel letter signed by the tenant before I
could close.

After closing, I contacted the tenants to let them know
we took over the property and wanted to update their

lease. We did this by sitting down to review the entire lease before signing. At the same time, I updated them on the repairs we were going to make to ensure they were living in a safe home. Shortly after, this family determined that they'd outgrown the home and moved out with proper notice.

The issue was that the family did not notify me until 3 days after that they had vacated the property. We secure vacant properties by posting No Trespassing signs and installing a security system. By the time we received possession, some neighborhood kids broke into the single wide and kicked in most of the drywall. Luckily for us, drywall was the only damage they did.

We always have a "whoops" budget for when the unexpected happens. It does not feel good to spend the extra money on repairs, but it didn't ruin the deal for us. *Always* have a larger rehab budget than you expect to need.

Key Takeaways

- Some sellers need time and multiple attempts before they'll sell.
- A personal referral is the strongest type of lead.
- Sit down and talk to the residents you take over.
- Always have a "whoops" budget for when things do not go as planned.

All right! What are you doing? You're turning to Chapter 17, aren't you?

To download go to **Lifestyle-rei.com/free-bonus**

Chapter 18. 1031 Exchange Purchase #6

A young wholesaler called me because he had a mobile home he wanted to wholesale. He explained that the property was in probate and no payment was made to the bank for years. The double wide belonged to a hoarder, and it was a known drug house. He also let me know it was a 1990 double wide on almost a quarter acre. Then he told me his asking price.

I was intrigued given that we had some 1031 money to spend. We walked the property. I thought, *wow, this would be the biggest project I've ever done.* The place needed at least ten, sixty-yard dumpsters of junk removed. It smelled like the dogs used the house like a fire hydrant, and the front door was missing. I gave the wholesaler the price I would buy at, which didn't work for him. He said that's less than his contract price with the seller.

A week later I asked if he'd found a buyer; to my surprise, he had not assigned the contract to another buyer. I recommended that he renegotiate with the seller. The seller helped us compromise by promising to remove all the trash if we raised our purchase price.

We had a deal! If the young wholesaler was not hungry to make money and do his first deal, this would never have happened. He did what it took to close this deal! He drove the adult son, who was living in the property, to the probate attorney's office. He ordered the dumpster for the seller to clean up, stopped by to motivate the seller to get things done, negotiated with the bank on the amount owed, and called me for advice when he got stuck. I'm sure he did more too. This is how deals are made!

It was time to close on this property, and as I'd learned earlier, I told title companies that I must have the documents three days before closing. My title company reviewed the work and sent back over ten items that were incorrect. Wow!

I informed the title company of the errors that needed to be fixed. I took a deep breath as I realized that I was preventing future problems. While my contractors were working on the property, people on the street thanked us for cleaning up this property. Buying and fixing up the worst home on the street is something I had read about but hadn't experienced.

I thought the correct rent for the two-bedroom, two-bathroom double wide was $800 a month, but I decided to ask some neighbors. I was not fearful of knocking on the doors of the neighbors because of a door knocking class I'd taken a few years prior. To my surprise, the neighbors said I should be charging $950 a month! I made an extra $150 a month by spending an hour talking to neighbors.

Now that the final transaction of the 1031 exchange was completed, we reflected and thought this 1031 exchange was a lot of work but worth every minute of effort. We changed our lives by increasing our net cash flow by almost $3,000 a month!

Key Takeaways

- Buying and fixing up a property can be about more than just money.
- When the seller will not drop the price, ask the seller to do some work.
- Going above and beyond is how you make a deal close.
- Utilize a team member, such as your regular title company, to prevent title work errors.

C'mon. You know what to do. Chapter 18. PDF companion. To download go to **Lifestyle-rei.com/free-bonus**

Chapter 19. How to Find Value

How to value a mobile home is a very common question. The short answer is the same way to find the value of any house—you look for comparable sales in the area. This can be tricky on homes older than 20 years and even more difficult on mobile homes manufactured before June 15, 1976. This is because bank financing does not exist in these older homes. To purchase these homes, the buyer needs cash, private money, or owner financing. These financing options change the purchase price. We'll look at the differences between these in a later chapter. For now, let's explore some methods to value a mobile home.

I've never had an appraisal done for a mobile home. This is mainly because I am purchasing for cash flow, not for resale value. I do want to make sure I have a backup or exit strategy if I find a property that isn't fit for me. You'll find homes older than 1980 have very little appraisal value even though they have a cash flow value to you as a housing provider and there is value of a roof over the head of the person living in the home.

If you do want to account for the land value, you'll need to look for comparable land sales. You do this by looking at the property appraiser's website and recently sold comparable land in the area. I don't like to invest with the goal of appreciation. If I feel a builder will want to purchase the land soon, I might pay a little more because I treat it like a "lotto" ticket. It is not recommended to buy at breakeven or negative cash flow for a lotto ticket.

A cash purchase is typically the lowest price offered to purchase. When you are looking at comparable properties, you need to not only compare the home but how the home is purchased. Your property appraiser's website should have this information available. If you plan to use cash, I suggest finding comparable properties that cash was used to purchase.

Mobile homes are sometimes financed by investors to homeowners. You will notice these investors sell the property at a price that is arguably higher than the actual value. The buyer is happy with the price because they can afford the monthly payments. In these cases, you must realize this is an inflated price. You can usually figure this out by reading who the mortgagee is in the mortgage documents for the lender. You might find the real price is somewhere between the cash price and the owner-financed price.

A quick side note: If you're thinking of selling with owner financing, I highly recommended talking to an attorney in your state that specializes in this. You should also read the Dodd-Frank Act (or SAFE Act) to ensure you are complying with the appropriate laws.

Key Takeaways

- Mobile homes can be valued the same as a site-built home.
- Mobile homes can be valued as an ROI.
- Do not forget to consider the land value associated with a mobile home.
- Seller financing might be an inflated price.

Do I have to say it? Do I really? Turn to Chapter 19 in your PDF companion for takeaways and photos. To download go to **Lifestyle-rei.com/free-bonus**

Chapter 20. Financing

There are several financing options when it comes to investing in a mobile home with land: cash, hard money, private money, and owner financing.

Cash

Cash is king! But it typically runs out, especially when you are in your Estate building phase. Although cash is technically not a financing tool, we have to make a decision about when is the right time to use our cash or to use someone else's cash.

I love having properties that are free and clear. This gives us the ability to relax when we have vacancies, have higher cash flow per month, and the ability to borrow money quickly if needed.

Hard money

Hard money is a common term for borrowing money on real estate. I have not personally used hard money for multiple reasons. First, it is more expensive than private money. Second, it's for short-term borrowing, and I invest for the long term. Third, most hard money lenders do not lend on mobile homes.

If you want to find a hard money lender for your mobile home, you'll need one that understands mobile homes. You can always educate them by showing examples of income you are receiving from a mobile home or giving them a copy of this book. If you decide to use hard money, make sure you ask about all of the fees. A benefit of using hard money is that your lender can be a second set of eyes. If a hard money lender refuses to lend on a property, ask why not. Use it as a learning experience.

Private money

Private money is funding lent to you from someone you personally know. This could be a friend, family member, coworker, etc. Not someone from social media with 12 in common friends. You want them to be reliable, and you want to make sure you comply with the SEC rules.

Owner payments don't work for every owner's life situation. And when we run out of cash, private money becomes the way to pay for the property. These are my rules when it comes to private money:

1. We (the lender and I) must trust each other.
2. We must both feel like we have the best side of the agreement.
3. We must have all the documents signed before money is disbursed.

At the end of the day, I want those lending me money to trust and understand my business to the point that they are willingly lending to me while also having the security of the real estate in case I suddenly die.

Why do I like private money? Because I am dealing with a human. If I am going to write a check every month, I feel much better knowing that I am helping Brian get a step closer to his retirement goals, or that I'm building up college funds for Kevin's kids.

In the rare event there was a problem, I want the option to sit down and talk to my private money lender and tell them exactly what's going on and ask for help. I don't feel like this is a conversation a bank representative will have with me because I tried that in 2008. I called Washington Mutual twice a day, every day for a month trying to work something out before I decided to stop the monthly bleeding and accepted a short sale.

I recently borrowed 80% of the purchase price of a mobile home with the land at 7% interest only for four years. This required small monthly payments to the private money lender, which allowed us to receive a larger monthly cash flow. My private money lender did not ask for an appraisal as he felt the purchase price was fair. He took into account the needed repairs and the amount of potential rent we would collect. These terms allowed us to pay a little more for the property because we will have higher cash-on-cash return. (We are investing for monthly cash flow, not appreciation.)

You must decide what returns and risks you are comfortable with. These are the numbers that worked for us at the time of this purchase.

Performance-based notes are another opportunity for friends to lend money on a property. We inform them of the buy-in amount, and they will receive half of the monthly *net* rent. This performance-based note doesn't have a specific interest rate. The payment is determined by the performance of the property. This structure enables you to leave closing with a check or only bring a small check to closing. The main determining factor on a performance-based note is the monthly cash flow return.

Many of my private money lenders want a prepayment penalty if paid off early. They request this because they are not in the business of lending money out every month. They value a monthly payment and when they are paid off early, their payment stops. A prepayment allows for the lender to plan in advance because they receive the prepayment penalty in place of the monthly interest.

Balloons can be dangerous! A *balloon* is when a lump sum of money from the mortgage or note is due at once. If you choose to borrow money with a balloon payment, it's not recommended that you have multiple balloon payments due in the same year. You'll also want to have a safe refinance option available. You might want to consider paying your balloon payment completely off with the cash you have been saving from your high cash flow.

How do you find private money lenders? You will find everyone can be a private money lender, and some are cheaper than others. One person might be after a 15% return, and some want a 6% return. Anyone can lend money to you.

You'll find that because mobile homes are at a lower price point, it's easier to find people with funds available. IRA accounts are wonderful to borrow money from. The account holder of the IRA will need to transfer their money to a true SDIRA to be a custodian that can lend you money.

Some insurance agents, attorneys, dentists, doctors, delivery drivers, etc. are striving for higher returns in their retirement accounts. A friend of mine said after a few years of his lawyer doing paperwork, the lawyer said, "I want to be a part of these rentals you own."

Members of mastermind groups are another great source of friends who can act as lenders. These people hear your biggest problems, observe your feedback, and months later, hear your report on how you've improved. This builds trust, which is one of the main ingredients needed for someone to lend you money.

Talking about your success with private money lenders can be a wonderful way to let your friends know you have great opportunities. The key factor is to prove you are successful and give people an opportunity to make a fair return.

When pursuing private money, remind yourself that you're offering an opportunity, not begging for money. Your private money lenders must trust you.

Owner financing

I have found mobile home owners are familiar with the idea of owner financing because many purchased their mobile home this way. I can pay their asking price if they allow me to make payments to them.

Here are some tips to get owner financing.

Don't call it owner financing. Financing sounds complicated, and it implies you are going to pay interest. I am not against paying interest, but I like to start the negotiation at 0%.

The phrase *payments* is better than *financing*.

I reply to the seller's asking price with "I can pay you that if I can make you payments." The most important part of this is to SHUT UP after you say this. It can be difficult to be quiet when you are uncomfortable asking for the first time. But trust me—if you have to wait for a reply, their response is most likely a no!

A common reply is "what would that look like?" Before I meet with the seller, I do some quick math to know the max I can pay per month and still be profitable. I get an idea for how much I'd want to put down as well from the mental picture the seller has painted over the phone. While I'm walking the property, I'm adjusting this down payment in my head.

I reply with something along the lines of "what would work for you?" We talk it through from there. I like to do this sitting down with paper so we can take notes. There are many times I sit there and think or write. If I need a few minutes to think over the number, I tell the seller that.

When we get to a sticking point, I've even told them I need to call my wife and talk it over. I go to my car, call my wife, and talk it through.

"How do we do this paperwork?" This is another common question I'm asked when pursuing owner financing. I always ensure the owner that the title company will take care of the paperwork. This usually makes them feel more comfortable: "The ladies at the title company are professionals at making sure all the paperwork is correct for everyone. That's what they do all day, so I leave it to them, and I stick to what I am good at."

Owner financing may require a bit more conversation and calculation, but it's still a viable option as you expand your portfolio.

Key Takeaways

- If a hard money lender says no, ask why not.
- Private money lenders are people who know and trust you (and vice versa).
- When making a lending request, you are giving an opportunity to private money lenders, not begging for money.
- Private money lenders are all around you if you tell people what you are doing.

You're getting there. Go ahead and turn to Chapter 20 in your PDF companion for takeaways and photos. To download go to **Lifestyle-rei.com/free-bonus**

Chapter 21. Mindset and Taking Action

Many people often question why I frequently mention mindset. The truth is that growing our investment portfolio required more than education—it required conscious effort and action! Ultimately, I had to apply a healthy, humble mindset to keep learning and pushing myself to grow in new ways.

I believe business is easy, but we get in our own way. There are many simple ways you can profit in business. If you copy someone that you believe to be successful, there's a 100% chance that you will be successful too.

So why are more people not successful? Because most people don't have the right mindset. The people I believe to be super successful all are on this never-ending journey of self-development. You must build your confidence to believe you can do anything. You don't need to choose between self-development or real estate education because you should do both.

Fear is what holds most of us back. Fear of failure. Fear of looking stupid. Fear of not being enough. Fear of _____ (you fill in the blank). I have found making baby steps to build confidence breaks down fear barriers one brick at a time. Building my confidence in public speaking, health, and athletics all carry over to me being more confident to make money in real estate. You may find it rewarding to use a part of your life you excel at to build your overall confidence and mindset.

When I was looking to expand my network and get outside of my comfort zone, I visited the Plant City Toastmasters club. I did not join to become a public speaker, but it was meant to be. Over my years of being involved in Toastmasters, I was at a training when someone said, "If we sell anything, we sell confidence."

Most people's biggest fear is public speaking. If you can tame or conquer your biggest fear others become easier to get control of. I would not have the confidence I have today without Toastmasters.

There is no one right person to follow when it comes to mindset because most people are saying the same thing with different words and stories. Some of my favorite people to follow are Teresa Nelson, Kathy Neubauer, Peter Kolat (Polish Peter), the late Chuck Bauman, Hal Elrod, Mel Robbins, and Jim Rohn.

But who you learn to grow from does not matter as much as choosing to grow your mindset. I follow these people, and many more, on social media, YouTube, podcasts, books, and live events. Visit Lifestyle-rei.com/mentors for an expanded list of my mentors.

Over 95% of people that attend real estate investing meetings never take action. Nothing in this book will help you if you do not take action! Although this book focuses on buying mobile homes with the land, there are many other ways to take action and profit in real estate. Private money lending, property management, or property locator are roles that add value to the transaction. There are many ways to participate in the profits of real estate investing if you open your mind and take action!

I believe in taking action and being willing to learn along the way. This is because we will never know it all! Those I believe to be the greatest investors still take classes, read books, and make mistakes. Find your comfort level for taking action, but I believe the best time to take action is when you think you know around 50 to 60% of what there is to know. Remember no one makes 100% of the shots they take!

You are proving to yourself that you can take action by reading this book. What will be your next course of action within the next month? The next week? The next day? The next hour?

If you're searching for a community to grow with others, I have the right one for you.

Visit **Lifestyle-rei.com/free-bonus** for more details.

Key Takeaways

- Fear holds most of us back.
- You must take action to succeed in real estate investing.
- Private money lenders, property managers, and property locators are important roles in real estate investing.
- No one will know it all, so be confident and know this is a commitment to lifelong learning and development.

Do you know what to do now? Turn to Chapter 21 in your PDF companion for takeaways and photos. To download go to **Lifestyle-rei.com/free-bonus**

Chapter 22. You can do it too

I believe that if you desire, you can become a successful, financially free mobile home investor. But don't take my word for it. Here's what a few of my students have said.

First, Jimmy took my course, "Cashing in on Mobile Homes." I reached out to Jimmy after he took the course for some feedback. I was curious what action he had taken. Jimmy said the course felt very hands-on, which confused me because we didn't touch any mobile homes. Jimmy further explained how the pictures, slides, and stories helped the course feel hands-on.

Like all businesses, when we ask for feedback, we get an opportunity to better our business. I learned from Jimmy the value of keeping the pictures in the course for the hands-on feel they give, and as a result, I leaned into this even more in "The Ultimate Mobile Home Blueprint."

Next, to become a better housing provider, I had to realize that sometimes a small detail to us makes a big difference to someone else . Heather attended my "Full-Time Landlord, Part-Time Work" course. Halfway through the course, she told me if she had taken it a few weeks earlier, one specific tip about the security system in the course would have saved her thousands of dollars.

Last, Greg took my "Cashing in on Mobile Homes" course. Greg was a part-time investor who ran a family business that was sucking the life out of him. Shortly after finishing my course, Greg had the confidence he needed to do what he truly wanted: follow his passion as a full-time real estate investor. He closed his family business to become that full-time real estate investor, giving him more time freedom!

He has since taken "The Ultimate Mobile Home Blueprint" to continue his education and grow his real estate business!

Jimmy, Heather, and Greg all got the right education and took action with what they learned. You can do it too!

For more inspiration visit **Lifestyle-rei.com/testimonials**

Chapter 23. Fix & Flip Red Flags

When it comes to knowing how to fix and flip mobile homes, there's no one better than my good friend Marc. He's the best mobile home fix-and-flipper I've ever met, which is partly why I bring him in to teach on the topic.

In my view, his great success is partly because he started out as a contractor working on mobile homes. These days, however, Marc invests in fix-and-flips and hires a contractor to do the work. He's done over 200 of these, and he isn't finished yet.

The other reason I decided Marc was the right person to teach on this topic is he runs a business very much in alignment with the Lifestyle REI vision. In other words, Marc runs his business; it doesn't run him. He keeps his personal life a priority by spending time with his family and especially his two beautiful daughters. He also enjoys traveling and fishing and makes a point to schedule time for the things he truly enjoys. This section draws heavily on Marc's expertise from my "The Ultimate Mobile Home Blueprint."

Are you thinking about doing a mobile home fix-and-flip? Here are five red flags to watch out for before you buy a fix-and-flip:

Fix & Flip Red Flag #1: Septic tanks

Mobile homes are more common in rural markets. It's common to find them just outside of the city limits with an acre or more of land. This means the property will most likely have its own septic system.

There are many kinds of septic systems, and because laws change in different markets, be sure to stay up to date with all codes. It's important to have the septic up to code because your end buyer won't be able to pass inspection without it.

The two main parts of the septic system are the tank and the leach beds. The waste flows in that order, slowly making its way back to Mother Nature.

Depending on the depth of the water table in your area, your septic system may need to be raised. This means extra dirt is brought to the site so the system can be above the normal ground level. Because of how they're designed and so the waste can flow against gravity, these systems always need a pump.

No matter which system you have, driving over the tank or the leach beds is likely to damage the system.

Finally, keep tree roots from growing within the septic system.

Fix & Flip Red Flag #2: No HVAC

Do people really live without air conditioning and heating?

Not often, but Marc and I have found it more common for mobile homeowners than traditional housing options to _not_ use central air conditioning. Most commonly, it's replaced with window units. However, it's good to keep in mind your end buyer's bank financing will most likely require a central air conditioning and heating system. Mobile home HVAC systems are typically called a "package unit." This is because the entire system is in one package outside, unlike most houses that have part of the blower system inside and the condenser system outside. If the HVAC system has not been used for a long time, you'll want to check the air ducts because they could need repairing or replacing as well.

Fix & Flip Red Flag #3: Wetlands and flood areas

Again, mobile homes are typically in rural areas, which increases the chance of flooding. This is not always obvious, however, because some flooding happens seasonally. Potential flooding does not automatically disqualify the property from being a fix-and-flip. Keep in mind, when it comes to your repair budget, you may either need to make special repairs or the end buyer may need to have special flood insurance.

This is important for you to be aware of because when a buyer pays more for additional insurance, they may not be able to afford as expensive of a mobile home.

Fix & Flip Red Flag #4: Private road agreements

Sticking with the theme of the rural market, sometimes mobile homes are on a private road. This won't disqualify an end buyer, but you need to be aware of what to *look* for to make sure the end buyer is clear to close!

Sometimes a signature is required by all the owners on the road, so you'll just need to get your door-knocking shoes on!

138

Fix & Flip Red Flag #5: Do-it-yourself homeowner repairs

Many homeowners are known for doing their own repairs, and believe it or not, sometimes these repairs aren't safe! We have found these DIY repairs are more common in mobile homes than traditional housing options.

That's why it's important during your conversations with the homeowner to ask them the right questions - so you get an idea of the quality of repairs you can't see. In some cases, the homeowner doesn't repair the mobile home themselves, but that doesn't always mean they hired a professional. Sometimes in exchange for doing some repairs, they'll trade a six-pack with a random person they met at the corner store. In either case, you need to always be on the lookout because these unpermitted, unsafe repairs could add thousands of dollars to your rehab budget and delay the closing. There's so much more to learn about the mobile home fix-and-flip business.

That's why I asked Marc to teach a portion of my courses, "Cashing in on Mobile Homes" and "The Ultimate Mobile Home Blueprint."

Together they are your ultimate course on investing in Mobile Homes. In it, Marc teaches you how to fix and flip mobile homes while I teach you how to fix and rent mobile homes. These courses are pure education with our passion to give you everything you need to become a successful mobile home investor! If you are ready to profit from this nice I have a special coupon for you...

Visit **Lifestyle-rei.com/fixandflip**

Chapter 24. In Park Deals

Let's talk about investing within a mobile home park, you don't own the land the mobile home is parked on. This is typically called "lot rent." This type of investment can have a very high return on investment, and yet it's still recession resistant, just like mobile homes with land. That's because there's much less competition. Plus, it takes less money up front to make money.

I've made a fantastic return on these types of deals and so have my students.

Will you be one to make a huge profit off this niche?

When it comes to a mobile home within a park, you must understand that the park owner and/or park manager makes all the rules. For example, they will be the one to approve your buyer or resident. You'll want to personally talk to the manager and/or owner for several reasons. The main one is to make sure they'll be easy to work with.

This can start out with a simple phone call asking, "Do you allow rentals?" If the answer is anything but no, I suggest meeting in person to build the right rapport. I always like to ask what their application requirements are plus what their process looks like. No matter what my process is, the new buyer will still need to qualify with the park.

In my course, "From Trailer to Treasure, Big Money in Small Deals," you'll learn exactly how to build deep relationships with park owners and managers so they can help make you rich, rather than cause you massive headaches.

When it comes to investing in mobile homes with lot rent, four common mistakes people make are:

1. Not understanding that the lot rent stays with the home, not the person,
2. not talking with the park manager or owner,
3. giving the buyer a signed title before making sure it's transferred,
4. and over-rehabbing.

Let's talk about finding the price to pay. My quick, back-of-the-napkin math to value a mobile home is, I want comparable homes and apartments nearby to rent for at least double the lot rent. I also want to be able to sell the mobile home on payments for at least my all-in cost.

Adding up the following four items will help deter-mine your all-in costs:

1. The purchase price of the mobile home,
2. any holding costs, including lot rent and/or debt,
3. all closing and transfer costs,
4. and any money put toward improving the property.

A very common exit strategy for mobile homes within the park is selling them with owner financing. This is commonly called "rent to own." When it comes to fixing and flipping a mobile home within a park, you really need to know what you're doing.

Because, for example, unless you look good in orange behind bars, you need to fully understand the SAFE Act, which is commonly referred to as Dodd Frank. Enacted in 2008, the SAFE Act is the Secure and Fair Enforcement for Mortgage Licensing Act.

It sets the standards for mortgage loan originators and requires licensing, education, and background checks. It was enacted to increase consumer safety and reduce fraud.

Let's switch gears and take a look at one of my student's deals. In high school, John started working with his parents as a handyman on their properties. They were teaching him the value of handiwork, the power of mobile homes, as well as the benefits it can have on his life.

After taking my course, they found a mobile home within a park to purchase. It was decided this would be John's first deal. They found it initially as a pending sale. But they didn't use its status as an excuse not to contact the seller.

It's a good thing they contacted the seller because the pending buyer kept extending the closing each week due to lack of funds. The seller needed almost $10,000, and John didn't have the funds either.

But luckily, he was finishing up a project for his parents, which meant he'd be receiving the funds soon. After the sale went through, John decided to do the labor himself, but he still needed money for the materials to complete the repairs.

His parents offered to pre-pay him for work on their next project. When it came time for John to get to work cleaning the place out, painting, replacing carpet, etc., John was able to stay within the rehab budget he created, which was important for him to be profitable.

He had a total of $16,000 in the property, including...
- $4,000 on materials,
- a little bit of holding costs,
- as well as some closing costs.

After the repairs were complete, it was time for him to sell! John listed it with a mobile home dealer, but nothing happened. The listing agent had encouraged him to list it for more than it could sell for, so they had to start dropping the price. As time went by, John was about to need to dip into his savings. So John told the listing agent if she didn't find a buyer by the end of the month, he would cancel with her!

She magically found a buyer and John made a NET profit of $7,300, which is a 45% return on his investment! <u>That's</u> the type of return on your money that will get you jumping out of bed in the morning!

After John rewarded himself with a vacation, he was out looking for his next opportunity. John's story proves that mobile homes ROCK!

They give us the benefit to be:
- Where we want
- When we want
- With whom we want!

Which I call lifestyle freedom!

Are in-park deals right for <u>you</u>?

There's been so much demand on this topic, I created a course dedicated to this niche <u>within</u> the niche of mobile homes. In "From Trailer to Treasure, Big Money in Small Deals," we go over:

- Marketing strategies
- **How** to buy
- **How** to sell
- **How** to collect monthly checks without the toilets and tenant phone calls
- Common mistakes and how to prevent them
- Golden nugget of **how** to use this niche to set yourself up to buy a mobile home park with owner financing
- **How** to qualify the park
- **How** to value the mobile home
- Multiple case studies!

Visit **Lifestyle-rei.com/inparkdeals** to find out more.

Chapter 25. What's Next?

We've covered a lot of information. By now you know...

1. about investing in mobile homes with the land to take action and change your future.
2. different ways to market to motivated sellers you can help.
3. what to look for when you are walking a mobile home.
4. differences between older and newer mobile homes.
5. about mobile home titles.
6. where to find insurance on mobile homes.
7. that cash flow is a major reason you invest in mobile homes with the land.
8. the importance of taking action.
9. red flags to look out for when fix & flipping
10. how to quickly calculate the numbers for an in park mobile home

Most importantly, you now know more than other investors in your market when it comes to investing in mobile homes!

The ball is in your court. Will you use this knowledge to help people and improve your life? Or will you pass this book on to someone that will?

Education is never-ending. The smartest people I know read books and attend classes on a regular basis. But education is not beneficial without action! I know you can become successful because I did it.

This journey is not as much about success as it is about having the lifestyle of freedom to be with family and friends when and where you want. I was the guy in the remedial classes in school, then I spent eight years paying college tuition to only obtain a two-year associate degree. I never got my real estate license. What I did do was find the right people to learn from, then I took action. You can do it too! If I can help, I will.

To connect and continue your education, visit **Lifestyle-rei.com/free-bonus**

Acknowledgments

We all are influenced by everyone that we interact with. Some people stay in our lives for a short time, others for a lifetime.

I mentioned some of my mentors when it comes to mindset, but I don't believe I would have started learning from each of them without my parents' guidance. My parents taught me so many things, but a few I take for granted are being open-minded, being different, and being loving and kind to everyone. If they had not instilled these core values or they hadn't told me I could be anything I wanted in life, I don't believe I would have been able to start my journey as a real estate investor.

My frequent visits to REIAs also helped me grow, but one in particular has made a huge impact on me: The Polk County Real Estate Investors. They have a very special leader as part of their group. She goes out of her way to do her part and make sure every single person that attends feels loved and welcomed. She wants the impossible—for everyone to be successful. She coached me to become a speaker and teacher before I realized what she was doing. Everyone needs a Lizzz in their life.

Masterminds have been a huge part of my success, importantly by the group of people I have the privilege to be surrounded by. My T4 family have been there to guide and support me along my journey. My T-shirt brand would not exist without the push that came from within T4. We started out as a mastermind group, but now we are family to support, hold accountable, and strategize about the future. I am years and maybe decades ahead because of T4.

A special thank you to the team at SelfPublishing.com for guiding me through the book writing journey.

Chandler Bolt has created an incredible resource that empowers everyday people to share their stories, and I am grateful to be one of them.

And to my coach Brett, your steady encouragement, clear direction, and accountability helped make this possible. Thanks for walking besides me every step of the way. You helped me turn ideas into impact!

I also want to thank Hal Elrod, *The Miracle Morning* became one of the foundations of my life, and for introducing me to Chandler and SelfPublishing.com

Funny how a morning routine can ripple into a published book.

And lastly, *thank you*, the reader. Whether this is your first step into mobile home investing or you're deep into the business, I appreciate your trust in me to guide you. To all my students, your wins, questions, and growth continue to inspire me. You're proof that freedom through real estate is possible, and I'm honored to walk this path with you.

About Me

I was born in Tampa, Florida, and raised in Plant City, Florida. My mom was an elementary school teacher until my younger brother was born. At that time, she stopped teaching to take care of us and help my father in the business he was building. My father is an immigrant from Argentina. He started selling plants, which developed into statue sales and creating custom wrought iron. I had a wonderful middle-class childhood, working in the business and learning how to be an entrepreneur.

In school, I was put in remedial classes because I was a slow reader. It took me four years in college to finish my two-year associate degree. I then spent another four years at University of South Florida without completing a degree. Even though school was a huge challenge for me I learned to never give up.

I worked in the kitchen of a restaurant for a few weeks, Walmart for a few years, and the YMCA for a few months. Each of these jobs taught me valuable lessons. I then started traveling the country setting up events for third-party marketing companies. I was paid to represent Fortune 500 companies while seeing our beautiful country with one of my best friends, Charlie. I knew this was not a forever job for me.

Later, I became a day trader in the stock market which only yielded me an awesome computer with four monitors without the income I'd hoped for. To my surprise, a lot of what I learned from the stock market has carried over into my time in real estate.

Today I am a full-time real estate investor, educator, and host a high-level real estate mastermind, Elite Level Mastermind. I teach about my successes and failures with the purpose of inspiring others to live the life of their dreams!

Want More?

My goal when it comes to education is passing on what I have learned from my mentors and experience.

I am teaching from my successes and failures as well as bringing in trusted colleagues to teach on topics where they hold special expertise.

The majority of this happens on Lifestyle-rei.com

And don't forget to follow Lifestyle rei on social media for tips and to stay up to date on future education.

Thank you for taking the time to read this book and trusting me with your education.

Love this book? Don't forget to leave a review!

Every review matters, and it matters a lot!

Head over to Amazon or wherever you purchased this book to leave an honest review.

I thank you endlessly